You Decide!
Making Responsible Choices

by Jean Bunnell

inside illustrations by Susan Kropa

cover illustration by Rick Clubb

Publisher
Instructional Fair • TS Denison
Grand Rapids, Michigan 49544

ISBN: 1-56822-427-3

You Decide!

Copyright © 1997 by Instructional Fair • TS Denison
2400 Turner Avenue NW
Grand Rapids, Michigan 49544

Table of Contents

About This Book

As students reach middle-school age, they assume more responsibility for their lives. Fewer decisions are made for them by adults; therefore, students get to make more choices. But making decisions is not always easy, and students are often poorly prepared. Often, there is conflict between young people and their parents, teachers, and other adults as this transition in decision-making power takes place.

Students need to learn skills that will aid them in making choices: identifying options, isolating various factors, exploring pros and cons, and predicting possible consequences. This book is designed to help students gain those skills.

Each lesson begins with a story. Someone in the story has a decision to make. Follow-up activities and activity sheets explore the decision. What factors will influence the decision? Is there a right decision? Why might one decision be better than another? How are facts a part of the decision making? How are feelings a part of the decision making?

Lessons included in this book cover a wide spectrum of decisions including health and safety concerns, relationships with family, relationships with friends, and quality-of-life decisions. Students are encouraged to look at their own lives and apply what they learn to their own real world.

Detailed information for the teacher also accompanies each lesson. There is an overview of the story situation, a listing of objectives, instructions for preparing the lesson, and guidelines for presenting the lesson to the class.

These lessons will serve as springboards to thoughtful discussion for you and your students.

A Swim at the Quarry

Overview
Sometimes people are tempted to do dangerous or risky things. And young people face those same temptations. Brad, Nick, and Joe are facing a long hot day with nothing much to do. Then, they remember the dangerous and forbidden quarry and contemplate going there for a cooling swim.

Objectives
1. Identify potential warning signals that an activity is dangerous.
2. List possible responses when being encouraged to do something risky or dangerous.

Preparation
Make one copy of each of the following pages of "A Swim at the Quarry" for each student:

> You Decide
> Activity Sheet
> Thinking It Over

Have copies of recent newspapers and magazines available.

Presentation
Talk with the class about taking dangerous risks. Perhaps a recent movie or TV show has portrayed someone considering or taking a foolish risk. Talk about what happened. Why do people take stupid chances?

Distribute copies of "Activity Sheet." Read to learn about some signals that can warn when a behavior is risky or dangerous. Talk about how these signals were evident in the movie or TV show discussed earlier.

Distribute copies of "You Decide." Ask students to watch for warning signals as they read the story. Read the story together.

Have students work alone or in pairs to complete the activity sheet.

Distribute copies of "Thinking It Over." Read together the newspaper article about the lost skier. Talk with students about what they would have done if they had been the friend with Bonnie Brown when she decided to ski the back side of the mountain. Why would they have known it was a dangerous risk? What would they have said and done? Have students continue to work on the page, completing it as homework if necessary.

During the next class period, discuss the newspaper articles collected by students. What were warning signs that these activities would be dangerous? How would they have responded in the situation?

You Decide

"Whew, I'm sweating," Brad sat down on the steps beside Nick.

"You're not the only one," agreed Nick who was sitting slumped down with his chin in his hands. Brad and Joe had come over to Nick's house, but the weather seemed too hot for doing much of anything.

"I've never been so hot!" complained Joe. He was sprawled on the lawn by the stairs. "We gotta go swimming."

"Yeah, sure," said Nick. "But where? And how are we going to get there?"

"Can't your mother take us to the lake?" Brad looked at Nick.

"No . . . her car's not working right so she can't drive it much. And anyway, she's got to work this afternoon."

"Too bad we can't go swimming at the pit," said Joe. The pit was an abandoned quarry several miles from Nick's house.

"Why can't we go?" asked Brad.

"They don't allow swimming there," responded Nick. "No one's been allowed to go there since the quarry closed. It's too dangerous."

"Who says? My brother's gone swimming there before," said Brad. "He said the water was super cold. That's just what we could use!"

"Yeah," said Nick. "But no one is supposed to swim there. They have a chain across the road. And there are signs that say NO SWIMMING."

"Did anybody catch your brother when he was swimming there? Did your brother get in trouble?" asked Joe.

"He just got in trouble with my parents. My mother says the rocks are slippery and jagged and you could fall and hit your head. Besides,

there's no telling what kind of things are left around from when they used to quarry there. They grounded my brother for a week."

"Your mother worries too much," said Joe.

"Nothing bad is going to happen to us," said Brad. "We can ride our bikes past the chain and no one will ever know we're there."

"How'd your parents find out your brother had been swimming at the pit?" asked Nick.

"He and his friends were joking around about it afterwards. And my dad overheard them."

"We'll be careful not to talk about the pit anywhere around our parents—and they'll never find out."

"I don't know." Nick hesitated. "What'll I tell my mom right now?"

"Tell her we're going over to my house," suggested Brad. "She'll let you do that."

"Yeah," said Joe, standing his bike up and getting ready to ride. "We've gotta do something to get cooled off. Let's go . . . ."

"I'm ready," said Brad. He turned to Nick. "Are you coming?"

Name _____

Activity Sheet

When people are thinking about doing something, there are often warning signals if it is foolishly risky or dangerous. Read the four warning signals listed below. In each box, tell how you see that warning signal in the story about Brad and Nick and Joe.

Warning Signal 1: People pretend there is no risk. They give examples of other people who have done this before. _____ _____ _____ _____ _____	Warning Signal 2: The activity is surrounded by secrecy and lies. _____ _____ _____ _____ _____
Warning Signal 3: It begins to seem like this is the only choice and these are special circumstances. _____ _____ _____ _____ _____	Warning Signal 4: Other people and friends push a person to do something that person feels is wrong. _____ _____ _____ _____ _____

Nick has a decision to make. When Brad and Joe invite him to come to the quarry with them, what should Nick say and do?

_____

_____

_____

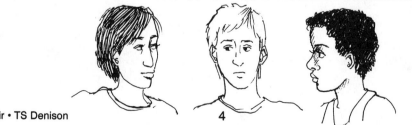

Thinking It Over

Read the following newspaper story. Then answer the questions.

Lost Skier Found

SKI TOWN—Bonnie Brown was cold and wet, but uninjured, when rescuers found her at 1:30 Thursday morning in a shallow snow cave less than 30 yards from a logging road. Brown had headed out alone the afternoon before on a back-country ski excursion. She had neither a map nor a guide and was without survival gear. "Basically, she violated almost every principle of back-country skiing," said officials at the resort. A friend of Brown, who had declined to join her in skiing off the back of the mountain, reported Brown missing at about 6 p.m. Wednesday. Rescuers searched into the night. Relatively mild conditions, with temperatures dropping only into the low 20s, helped avoid a tragedy.

1. What shows Bonnie Brown was taking a dangerous risk to ski the back side of the mountain?

   _____

   _____

   _____

2. If you had been Bonnie's friend with her on the mountain, what would you have said or done when Bonnie told you about her plan to ski the back of the mountain?

   _____

   _____

   _____

3. Look through the newspaper to find a story of someone doing something foolishly risky or dangerous. Tell about the situation. If you had been there, what would you have done?

   _____

   _____

   _____

   _____

4. Think of a time in your own life when you or a friend considered doing something risky or dangerous. Tell about the situation. What happened?

   _____

   _____

   _____

   _____

5. Looking back, how do you think it could have been handled better?

   _____

   _____

Full Pockets

Overview

Smoking has been proven dangerous to our health, but millions of people continue to smoke. Kayla discovers that her brother is smoking and reveals this information to the family. Although their father is a smoker, he does not want his children to smoke.

Objectives

1. List some of the many choices made by people in the story "Full Pockets."
2. Survey adult smokers to learn about their experience.
3. Identify "good" and "bad" reasons for smoking.

Preparation

Make one copy of each of the following pages of "Full Pockets" for each student:

You Decide	Survey Sheet
Activity Sheet	Thinking It Over

Presentation

Day 1

Talk with students about why people smoke. What reasons do they suggest that people smoke? Make a list on the board.

Distribute copies of the story "You Decide." There are three STOP signs throughout the story. Instruct students to ignore these for now and read the story through from beginning to end. Talk briefly with the class about events in the story.

Distribute copies of "Activity Sheet." Now ask students to go back through the story to see how many people made choices that affected this story. Have students work individually or in pairs to complete the activity sheet. Talk about the different choices that people could have made.

OPTIONAL ACTIVITY: Choose one STOP sign. If a different choice is made here, how might the story be changed? Write the rest of the story. Students can choose any STOP sign and choice they prefer. Have students share their stories.

Conduct a survey of some people who smoke. Distribute copies of "Survey Sheet." Talk with students about the questions. Have students complete the survey as homework.

Day 2

Compile the results of the survey. Does the class find any patterns? What is the most common reason for smoking? What is the most surprising reason? How many people would smoke again if they could live their lives over? Did the pool of people surveyed "weight" the results in any particular direction?

Distribute copies of "Thinking It Over." Have students answer the questions. Discuss their answers.

You Decide

"What's for dessert?" John asked as he swallowed his last bite of baked potato. "How about some pie?"

"No, there's no pie in the house," answered his mother. "In fact there's not much of anything for dessert unless one of you kids wants to get some ice cream."

"I'll go." Kayla jumped up from the table. The convenience store was just three blocks away. She could get there quickly on her bicycle.

Kayla spotted John's denim jacket lying across the end of the couch. "O.K. if I wear your jacket?" Kayla asked.

"Why don't you wear your own?"

"Mine's upstairs in my room. This will be quicker."

 **STOP #1**

"Yeah, O.K., you can wear it," John agreed grudgingly.

"I won't hurt your old jacket," said Kayla as she slipped her arms in the sleeves and then zipped up the front.

"Will you please get chocolate chip ice cream?" Molly pleaded with her older sister.

"We always get chocolate chip; let's have strawberry for a change," suggested Kayla.

"You get whatever flavor you think we'd all like," said Kayla's dad as he handed her some money. "This should pay for it . . . and don't forget to bring back some change!"

"Thanks, Dad." Kayla took the money and put it in her pocket. But the pocket was full. Kayla put her hand in the other pocket and it, too, was full. Kayla looked at John and his eyes met hers.

 **STOP #2**

Kayla hesitated a moment. Then she pulled her left hand out of the pocket. "What are these doing in your pocket?" she asked. In her hand were two cigars and a package of cigarettes. Then she pulled her right hand out of the pocket. She held up a pipe and smoking tobacco.

The room was silent. People looked at what Kayla was holding and then they looked at John. John stared angrily at Kayla and then slowly turned toward his father.

"What's the story?" John's father asked him. "What's all this doing in your pockets?"

"We were just trying it, some of us guys. We wanted to see what smoking is like . . . ."

"I've told you it's a nasty habit and I don't want you smoking. Where'd you get all these cigarettes and cigars?"

"They're yours, Dad. I know you say I shouldn't smoke, but you do. It can't be all that bad."

 **STOP #3**

"You want to smoke? Well let's sit right here and do some smoking. Hand me those cigarettes, Kayla. Have a cigarette, son, and then another. Then smoke a cigar. Let's just sit here and smoke all evening. And put away that jacket, Kayla. We're skipping dessert tonight."

Activity Sheet

In the story about John and Kayla, there are several times when people make choices and those choices decide what will happen in a situation.

1. Read the story again as far as STOP #1. Then answer these questions.

   Who has a choice to make? _____

   What are two choices the person can make?

   Choice 1: _____

   Choice 2: _____

2. Continue reading the story as far as STOP #2. Then answer these questions.

   Who has a choice to make? _____

   What are two choices the person can make?

   Choice 1: _____

   Choice 2: _____

3. Continue reading the story as far as STOP #3. Then answer these questions.

   In some situations, several people have the opportunity to make choices. Who could make choices here? What might they do?

   Possibility #1: _____

   _____

   Possibility #2: _____

   _____

   Possibility #3: _____

   _____

Full Pockets
Survey Sheet

Talk with three adults you know who smoke. Tell them you are doing a survey for school and would like to ask them some questions. Write their answers to the following questions.

	Why do you smoke?	How did you get started smoking?	If you had your life to live again, would you smoke? Why or why not?
Adult #1			
Adult #2			
Adult #3			

Thinking It Over

1. Think about the story "Full Pockets." What reason does John give for wanting to try smoking?

   _____

2. John's dad told John not to smoke, but John smoked anyway. As the story ends, he invites John to join him for an evening of smoking. What do you think John's dad wants to happen?

   _____

   _____

   _____

3. Do you think this could be successful? Why or why not? _____

4. If John's dad asked you for advice about how to prevent John from smoking, what advice would you give him? Explain your thinking.

   _____

   _____

   _____

5. Think about the survey your class did. What did people say when asked, "Why do you smoke?" List some of the reasons given.

Reasons for Smoking

6. Will you make a choice to smoke? _____ Why or why not? _____

   _____

   _____

Fuel for Living
TEACHER INFORMATION

Overview

What fuel we use to provide for our bodies is a decision we make over and over. Sugar- and fat-laden foods taste good and frequently lure us away from healthier choices. Follow Stephanie through her day as she makes choices about how to feed her body.

Objectives

1. Identify foods in each category of the food pyramid.
2. Compare personal eating habits with Stephanie's eating habits.
3. Use nutrition information on packages to compare two snacks.
4. Plan a day of good healthy eating.

Preparation

Make one copy of each of the following pages of "Fuel for Living" for each student:

You Decide   Activity Sheet

Food Pyramid   Thinking It Over

Have available old magazines, scissors, glue, and poster board (optional).

Presentation

Day 1

Talk with students about what they have had to eat so far during the day. What are healthy foods? Have they made healthy choices? Why is it important to choose healthy foods?

Distribute copies of "You Decide." Read the story together. Ask which students identify with any part of the story: Who skips breakfast? Who has a chocolate bar and soda for quick energy? Who prefers chips and pizza over vegetables and fruit? Who picks at meals because they are full from snacking?

Distribute copies of "Food Pyramid" for students to use as a guide as they work alone or in pairs to make a food pyramid collage. Talk about the different food groups. Have students go through old magazines to find pictures of a variety of foods and glue them on a larger piece of poster board to make a collage.

Assignment: Ask students to keep a list of foods they eat during the next 24 hours.

Day 2

Distribute copies of "Activity Sheet." Recommendations from the food pyramid are in the center of the page. Have students list Stephanie's food choices in the appropriate blocks on the left of the page and list their food choices on the right.

Distribute copies of "Thinking It Over." Have students answer the questions. After completing the paper, students can meet with a partner for feedback about choices made.

You Decide

"STEPH - ANNNNN - EEEEEEEEE!"

Hearing her name, Stephanie stirred in her bed. She forced open her eyes to study her alarm clock—7:42.

"DO YOU HEAR ME, STEPHANIE? IT'S TIME TO GET UP!" The voice was her mother's.

"Yeah, I'm coming." Stephanie hoped her mother would stop yelling. She pulled herself out of bed and headed for the bathroom.

Ready for school 15 minutes later, Stephanie ran down the stairs, grabbed her jacket and books, and headed for the door.

"Good morning. Come have some breakfast," her mother urged Stephanie. "Cereal and a glass of juice won't take too long."

"I've gotta go," insisted Stephanie. "The bus comes at eight." And she dashed out the door.

During mid-morning recess, the student council at Stephanie's school operates a small store where they sell food and school supplies. Stephanie was hungry after two classes and went to the store. "I'll have this chocolate bar and a cola." She paid for her purchases and ate them during recess.

At lunch, Stephanie ate the slice of cheese pizza and potato chips on her lunch tray. "Do you want your carrot and celery sticks?" asked her friend Anne, who was sitting across the table.

"Nah . . . you can have them," said Stephanie. "And you can have my orange, too. It's too hard to peel."

It was nearly 3:30 when the school bus dropped Stephanie at her house. Anne came home with her to work on their science project. "I'm hungry," complained Stephanie as they dropped their books on a kitchen chair.

"Me too," agreed Anne. "What's to eat?"

Stephanie searched the cupboards but did not find much. "There's some old oatmeal cookies— here have some." Stephanie passed the package to Anne and then took a couple for herself. "There's a package of chocolate chips. Hey . . . want to make some cookies?"

"That's a great idea. Will your mother mind?"

"Not as long as we clean up the baking dishes before she gets home."

It was nearly 5 o'clock by the time they finished baking and cleaning up the kitchen. "These are perfect," said Anne. "They're all warm and gooey—just the way I like them." They put some cookies on a plate and took it with them upstairs to Stephanie's room.

A little after six, Stephanie's mother and little brother arrived home. Her mother called upstairs, "Come down and set the table for supper. I brought some chicken. We've got to hurry; I have a meeting tonight."

The girls came downstairs. "Hi, Mom," Stephanie greeted her mother. "I'll just set the table for you and Craig. Then Anne and I will just take a little chicken upstairs to eat while we study."

"I don't know," said Stephanie's mother. "It won't hurt you to take a little time out. Eat with us and have a good supper."

"No," said Stephanie, taking a drumstick and heading for the stairs. "I'm not very hungry and we have to keep working."

Her mother called after her, "Steph - annn - eeee!"

Fuel for Living
Food Pyramid

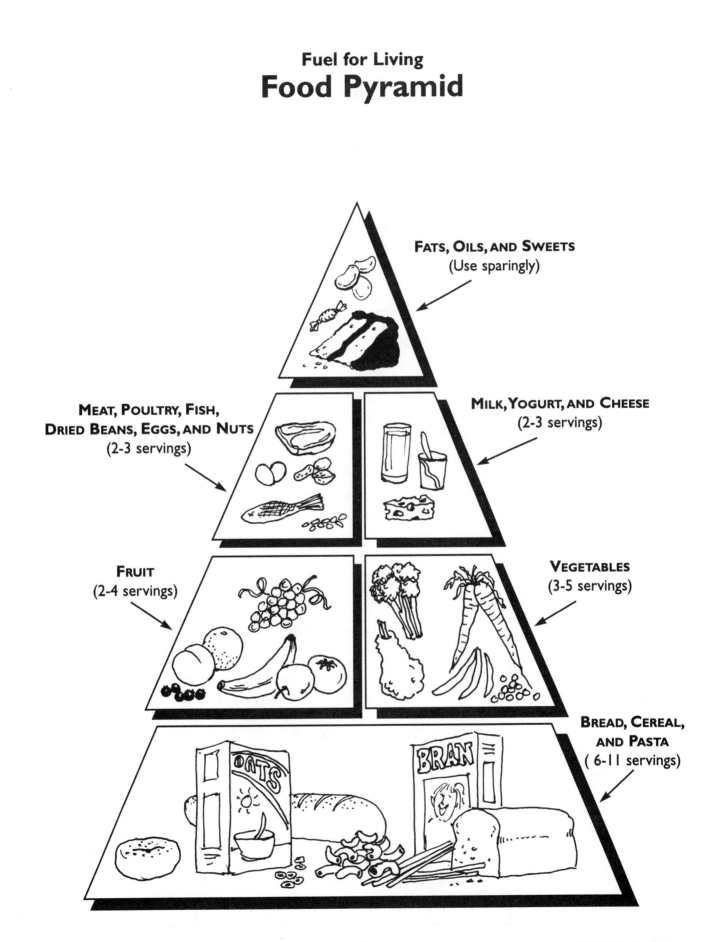

FATS, OILS, AND SWEETS
(Use sparingly)

**MEAT, POULTRY, FISH,
DRIED BEANS, EGGS, AND NUTS**
(2-3 servings)

MILK, YOGURT, AND CHEESE
(2-3 servings)

FRUIT
(2-4 servings)

VEGETABLES
(3-5 servings)

**BREAD, CEREAL,
AND PASTA**
(6-11 servings)

Name _____

Activity Sheet

Stephanie's Fuel for Living	Suggested Daily Fuel for Living	Fuel for Living I ate yesterday
	BREAD, CEREAL, & PASTA GROUP (6-11 servings recommended)	
	VEGETABLE GROUP (3-5 servings recommended)	
	FRUIT GROUP (2-4 servings recommended)	
	MILK, YOGURT, & CHEESE GROUP (2-3 servings recommended)	
	MEAT, POULTRY, FISH, DRIED BEANS, EGGS, & NUTS GROUP (2-3 servings recommended)	
	FATS, OILS, & SWEETS (use sparingly)	

Name _____

Thinking It Over

1. Packaging on most foods contains nutrition information. Compare the nutrition facts between these pretzels and these potato chips.

Pretzels

Nutrition Facts
Serving Size: 28g/About 10 pretzels
Servings Per Container: About 2

Amount Per Serving
Calories 110   Calories from Fat 0

% Daily Value

Total Fat 0g	0%
Saturated Fat 0g	0%
Cholesterol 0mg	0%
Sodium 340mg	14%
Total Carbohydrate 23g	8%
Dietary Fiber 1g	3%
Sugars less than 1g	

Protein 3g

The food pyramid suggests we use only small amounts of fats, oils, and sweets. How many grams of fat are in a serving of the potato chips? _____

How many grams of fat are in a serving of the pretzels? _____

How many grams of sugar are in a serving of the potato chips? _____

How many grams of sugar are in a serving of the pretzels? _____

Potato Chips

Nutrition Facts
Serving Size: 1 package
Servings Per Container: 1

Amount Per Serving
Calories 270   Calories from Fat 160

% Daily Value

Total Fat 18g	27%
Saturated Fat 5g	25%
Cholesterol 0mg	0%
Sodium 320mg	13%
Total Carbohydrate 25g	8%
Dietary Fiber 2g	6%
Sugars 0g	

Protein 3g

Which of these two products is a healthier snack? _____

2. Plan a healthy day of eating. What would you like to eat for each meal? For snacks? Be certain you eat the recommended number of servings from each food group.

	Bread, Cereal, and Pasta	Vegetables	Fruit	Milk, Yogurt, and Cheese	Meat, Poultry, Fish, Dried Beans, Eggs, and Nuts	Fats, Oils, and Sweets
Breakfast						
Lunch						
Dinner						
Snacks						
Your Totals						
Recommended number of servings	6-11	3-5	2-4	2-3	2-3	little

To Buy or Not to Buy

TEACHER INFORMATION

Overview

Gabe and Charlie are good friends. They study together and play sports together. One day Gabe tells Charlie that he is thinking about experimenting with drugs. Charlie is horrified and wants to talk his friend out of this idea.

Objectives

1. Research a variety of recreational drugs.
2. Identify people to talk with when wanting or needing help.
3. Plan an anti-drug lesson suitable for presenting to third graders.

Preparation

Make one copy of each of the following pages of "To Buy or Not to Buy" for each student:

You Decide	Drug Research
Activity Sheet	Thinking It Over

Presentation

Day 1

Talk with students about drugs. What do they know about drugs? What do they think about using drugs and about people who use drugs?

Distribute copies of "You Decide." Read the story together. Talk with students about how each of the characters might have been feeling during this conversation. What were the characters thinking and feeling at the end of their conversation?

Distribute copies of "Activity Sheet." Ask students to suggest people Charlie might want to talk with after his conversation with Gabe. Have students work alone or in pairs to write a dialogue.

ASSIGNMENT: Distribute copies of "Drug Research." Talk with students about stimulants, depressants, and hallucinogens. Ask each student to choose a drug and research that drug.

Day 2

Have students share with the class information they learned in their research.

Distribute copies of "Thinking It Over." Talk with students about the importance of having adults they can talk with about important matters. Ask students to think about who those adults are for each of them.

Students can work in pairs to prepare "drug lessons" they might teach to a third-grade class. If it is a possibility, make arrangements for some of the students to actually teach their lessons to a third-grade class.

You Decide

"This is boring," Gabe muttered as he pushed his book aside and looked across the table at Charlie.

"Yeah, you can say that again," Charlie whispered to Gabe as he kept on reading. The boys were in the library for a study hall.

"So why do you keep reading it?" Gabe asked.

"We've got to read it sometime, and we have hockey practice after school." Charlie went back to reading.

Gabe picked up his book but sat staring into space. After a while, he whispered to Charlie again, "Do you know Jim is into drugs?"

"Jim? Jim Hogan?"

Gabe nodded.

"No," scoffed Charlie. "That's not possible!" Jim played hockey with Gabe and Charlie. He was one of the best players.

"How do you know?" Charlie asked, his voice rising.

"Don't you gentlemen have any work to do?" The boys looked up to find the librarian, Mrs. Wagner, standing by their table. "This is a place for work; let's have it quiet in here."

Gabe and Charlie both returned to their books, and Mrs. Wagner went back into her office. When she was safely out of earshot, Charlie asked again, "How do you know Jim is doing drugs?"

"He offered me some this morning . . . on the bus," said Gabe.

"What did he have?" demanded Charlie.

Gabe was surprised by his friend's intensity. "Don't get all worked up," said Gabe. "It was pills—speed. He said he got them out of the medicine cabinet. They're his mother's. Jim said I could have as many as I wanted for $2 each. He said there are plenty more if I want more."

"You didn't take any, did you?"

"No," answered Gabe, "I didn't. I told Jim I'd have to think about it."

"Think about it? What's to think about?"

"Shhh . . . or she'll be back after us," said Gabe, nodding his head in Mrs. Wagner's direction.

Charlie lowered his voice and repeated his question. "What do you have to think about?"

"I don't know. What's the big deal? Everything's going OK for Jim—look, he's on the honor roll and playing sports. It's not going to hurt anybody if I pop a few pills."

"How do you know Jim's using?" asked Charlie. "Maybe he's just selling to get some money, and he's trying to talk you into helping him make money."

"You don't know that," said Gabe. "It's no big deal. Jim's not trying to make me into a druggie or anything. It's just a little fun."

"So are you going to do it?" asked Charlie.

"I don't know. I told you—I'm thinking it over."

Activity Sheet

In the story, "To Buy or Not to Buy," you read a conversation between Gabe and Charlie. Because Charlie was troubled by his conversation, he might want to talk with someone else. Read the following questions and answer them.

1. Charlie might talk with Jim.
   What are some things Charlie might want to say to Jim?

   _____

   _____

   _____

   How might Jim feel and respond to what Charlie would say to him?

   _____

   _____

   _____

2. Charlie might talk with his hockey coach.
   What are some things Charlie might say to his hockey coach?

   _____

   _____

   _____

   How might his hockey coach respond to Charlie's concerns?

   _____

   _____

   _____

3. Are there any other people with whom Charlie might want to talk?

   _____

4. Choose one pair of characters and write the dialogue for a conversation they might have. Use the back of this paper for writing your dialogue.

To Buy or Not to Buy
Drug Research

Stimulants speed up peoples' bodies; they make them feel peppy.
Examples: caffeine (in coffee, cocoa, tea, or soft drinks), cocaine, crack, amphetamines (uppers)

Depressants slow people down; they make them feel relaxed.
Examples: alcohol, sleeping pills

Hallucinogens cause people to see and hear things that do not exist.
Examples: marijuana, LSD, PCP

Choose one drug to research. Use books, pamphlets, or an encyclopedia to find information about that drug.

Drug: _____ Stimulant, Depressant, or Hallucinogen? _____

History: Where does it originate? How is it made? When was it first used?

Why would people want to use this drug?

What are the negative aspects of this drug?

Thinking It Over

1. Charlie might have wanted to talk to an adult about the conversation he had with Gabe. What characteristics do you look for in a person with whom you want to talk about something important? _____

_____

If you need to talk, who are the people you can trust to help you?
Write names in each of the following categories:

Relatives: _____   People at School: _____

_____   _____

Religious Leaders: _____   Others: _____

_____   _____

2. You and a friend have been asked to talk with the third graders about drugs. You have ten minutes for your presentation. Make plans for your time with the class.

What is your goal? What do you want the third graders to learn about drugs? Use the back of this paper if you need more room.

_____

_____

_____

3. Make up a slogan to use with your lesson.

_____

_____

_____

4. What will you tell the class about drugs?

_____

_____

_____

5. What activities (art work, theater, activity sheet, creative writing, etc.) will you do with the class?

_____

_____

_____

What's in the Backpack?

TEACHER INFORMATION

Overview
In a world increasingly filled with violence, we should not be surprised to find guns and weapons infiltrating our schools. Dale brings a pellet gun to school. It has been discovered. Dale and Dale's mother are meeting with the principal.

Objectives
1. Identify feelings behind specific body language.
2. Debate whether or not backpacks should be allowed in classrooms.
3. List appropriate consequences for inappropriate behavior.

Preparation
Make one copy of each of the following pages of "What's in the Backpack?" for each student:

You Decide	Debate Preparation
Activity Sheet	Thinking It Over

Presentation
Day 1
Distribute copies of "You Decide." This dialogue is presented like a play. Choose three students to read the parts of Dale, Mrs. Fisk, and the principal. Read (or assign another student to read) the few stage directions as they appear. Ask students to listen particularly to the character of Dale. How do they think Dale would be feeling and acting in this situation?

Divide the class into groups of three. Talk with students about feelings Dale might have been experiencing. Distribute copies of "Activity Sheet." Have students work together to complete the activities. (Note: Dale can be either a boy or a girl; "Mrs. Fisk" can easily become "Mr. Fisk.")

Have each group of three students present their dialogues. Can other students identify the feelings each character is trying to portray? How are the principal and Mrs. Fisk feeling?

This situation brings up a side issue of students bringing backpacks to their classrooms. If Dale had not been carrying a backpack, there might not have been a way to conceal the gun and bring it to school. Distribute copies of "Debate Preparation." Talk with students about the format of a debate (Affirmative Statement, Opposing Statement, Affirmative Rebuttal, Opposing Rebuttal, Affirmative Summary, Opposing Summary). Divide the class into two groups and have them prepare a debate. Each side will select three people to make speeches. Have students complete their debate preparation as homework.

Day 2
Students present their debate. Discuss the arguments presented. Which side presented the most convincing case? With which side do students agree? (They do not have to agree with the same side.)

Distribute copies of "Thinking It Over." If students could take the place of the principal, how would they handle this situation with concerned parents?

You Decide

Principal: [*Enters office with a student and the student's mother right behind him*] You sit over there, Dale. Mrs. Fisk, you can sit there. Now, tell me, Dale, what's been going on this morning with you at school?

Mrs. Fisk: DALE has never done anything like this before. Dale is an excellent student. I . . . .

Principal: Please, Mrs. Fisk. I'm talking to Dale. I want to hear what Dale has to say. [*Turning back to Dale*] I asked you a question—what's been going on this morning?

Dale: Nothin' much.

Principal: That's not what I hear from your teacher and some of the other students. They say you brought a gun to school.

Dale: It was just a pellet gun.

Principal: I don't care what it shoots. You brought a gun to school—and that's not allowed.

Dale: Nobody got hurt.

Principal: But somebody could have been hurt and . . . .

Mrs. Fisk: For crying out loud, Dale didn't have any ammunition!

Principal: That's enough, Mrs. Fisk. I asked you not to interrupt. If you can't be quiet, I'll have to ask you to wait outside. [*Turning again to Dale*] Why would you bring a gun to school?

Dale: I was just hackin' around.

Principal: I understand you told other students you were going to shoot your teacher. Is that what you call "hacking around"?

Dale: I was just kidding . . . . They don't know how to take a joke.

Principal: This is no joke, Dale. It's a very serious matter. And you are in serious trouble. Now tell me what happened.

Dale: It was in my backpack.

Principal: What was?

Dale: A pellet gun.

Principal: And did you show it to other students on the playground before school?

Dale: Yeah, I guess . . . just a couple of them.

Principal: And what did you tell them?

Dale: I didn't say anything much.

Principal: Is it true you threatened to use the gun on them if they reported you?

Dale: It doesn't even shoot without pellets and an air cartridge!

Principal: So why did you bring it?

Dale: I don't know . . . .

Principal: Whatever the reason, you made a big mistake, Dale. And your actions have consequences. For now, you are suspended from school. The police will be investigating. You and at least one of your parents will be expected to come to the school board meeting next Tuesday. Further decisions will be made then. Do you understand?

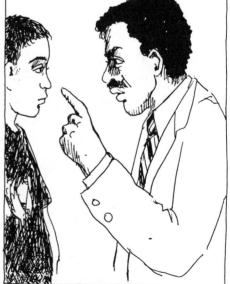

Dale: Yeah, I guess.

Principal: Do you understand, Mrs. Fisk?

Mrs. Fisk: We'll be at the meeting.

Principal: Since there's nothing more to discuss, let's end this meeting. I've got a school to run.

Name _____

Activity Sheet

A. In the story, "What's in the Backpack?," Dale brought a gun to school. Think about what might be happening in Dale's life. What possible reasons could Dale have had for packing a pellet gun in the backpack?

B. We can often see how people are feeling by the way they behave. An angry person and a happy person may both say the same words, but their actions show very different feelings. The unhappy person might scowl, speak softly, and seem withdrawn. The happy person might be smiling, speak politely, and behave in a friendly manner.

Think about how Dale might be feeling. Perhaps Dale is angry or afraid or ashamed. How will Dale's actions show those feelings? Beside each different feeling, describe behaviors in Dale that would show those feelings.

Feelings	Actions/Behaviors
angry	
afraid	
ashamed	

C. How do you think Dale was feeling? Act out the dialogue. Be certain each character's actions reflect his or her feelings.

What's in the Backpack?
Debate Preparation

In some schools, there is great concern about students carrying backpacks. Some people worry that backpacks can be used for carrying guns, knives, or other weapons. Others are concerned that drugs are being carried in backpacks. Some even claim that the weight of heavy backpacks can be damaging to students whose skeletal structures are still growing.

Prepare for a debate on this issue.
RESOLVED: *Students should not be allowed to bring backpacks to their classrooms.* (All backpacks must remain with students' coats or in their lockers.) Make a list of reasons you agree with this resolution (AFFIRMATIVE) and a list of reasons you do not agree with this resolution (OPPOSING).

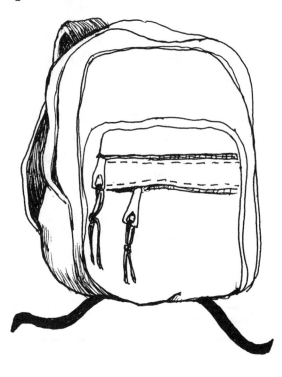

Affirmative	Opposing

Choose one side of the debate (either AFFIRMATIVE or OPPOSING) and write a speech explaining your position. Use the other side of this paper for your speech. (Important: It is not necessary to agree with the side of the debate you are arguing.)

Name _____

What's in the Backpack?

Thinking It Over

Assume you are the school principal. Parents are starting to hear about the "gun incident" at your school. You decide to write a letter to all parents. What will you say? What are the facts you wish to tell? What is your school policy concerning such an incident? What is being done about this situation? What will be done to make certain students at your school are safe?

Dear Parents,

_____

_____

_____

_____

_____

_____

_____

_____

_____

_____

_____

_____

_____

_____

_____

_____

Sincerely,

_____

School Principal

Let's Go Shopping
TEACHER INFORMATION

Overview

Stress is a reality in our lives today, and stressful situations also exist for middle school students. Stress can come from school activities, from the pressure to "fit-in," or from events at home. Kelly is puzzled by her friend's behavior and then discovers Fran is in the middle of a stressful situation.

Objectives

1. Recognize behaviors that may indicate stress.
2. Identify potential causes of both good and bad stress.
3. List healthy ways of responding to stress.

Preparation

Make one copy of each of the following pages of "Let's Go Shopping" for each student:

    You Decide   Stress Survey
    Activity Sheet   Thinking It Over

Have available: chalkboard and chalk, poster board, and markers

Presentation

Day 1

Talk with students about stress. What is stress? How do they behave when they are experiencing stress?

Distribute copies of "You Decide" and "Activity Sheet." Have students read the story and then answer the questions on "Activity Sheet." When most have finished writing, discuss the questions together.

Divorce is common today. It is likely that many students have had first-hand experience with the stress caused by divorce. Talk with students about other causes of stress. What do they think are the most common sources of stress? What have they found to be good methods of dealing with stress? What are their "stress-busters"?

Conduct a school survey to find the "top ten causes of stress" and the "top ten stress-busters." Distribute copies of "Stress Survey." Talk with students about good ways to ask questions. (Students each answer the survey themselves as student #1.) Assign the completion of the survey as homework.

Day 2

Compile the results of the survey. Use the chalkboard to write various causes of stress and stress-busters as reported by students. Tally totals beside each listing to determine the "top ten" in each category. Have two groups of students make posters of these lists.

Distribute copies of "Thinking It Over." Have students answer the questions. Discuss their answers.

You Decide

"Hey, Fran, wait up . . . ." Kelly ran after her friend. "Fran, I want to talk with you . . . ." Catching up with Fran, she grabbed her arm and they both stopped.

Kelly caught her breath. "You were in a hurry," said Kelly. "I didn't think I'd be able to catch up to you."

"I'm busy," snapped Fran. "And I've got to get home. What do you want?"

"Don't get ugly . . . . I just wanted you to go shopping with us—Sally and Jess and me. Sally's mom said she'd take us to the mall tomorrow afternoon. Will you come?"

"No, probably not," said Fran, turning to continue on her way.

"Well, why not?" asked Kelly.

"I just don't want to," Fran muttered over her shoulder.

"You used to like shopping! Now you don't want to do anything." Kelly started to shout as Fran continued to walk away. "We don't study together or talk on the phone. We used to be best friends and now you won't even talk to me at school. You're just being snobby and mean!"

Fran stopped debating what to do. Then she whirled around. "It's different now. Everything's different. Do you understand?"

"No, I don't understand!" Kelly was surprised by her friend's outburst. "What's different?"

Tears filled Fran's eyes.

"What is it? What's wrong?" Kelly's voice softened as she walked toward Fran.

"It's my parents . . . ," said Fran slowly. She brushed away the tears that were sliding down her cheeks. "They've been fighting a lot. They're . . . ." Fran hung her head. "They're getting a . . . divorce."

"Oh," said Kelly. "That's awful!"

"My dad moved out two weeks ago. Now it's just my mom and my brothers and me. My mom cries a lot. She really misses my dad."

"What are you going to do?"

"I don't know what's going to happen to us." Fran tried to stop crying. She juggled her books in her arms as she tried to wipe her face. "I think about it all the time."

Kelly tried to sympathize with her friend and said the first thing that popped into her mind. "When Sally's parents got a divorce, they had to sell the house and move. Now they live in an apartment and she has to share a bedroom with her sister."

"I know that, Kelly! You don't need to remind me!"

"Well, you can still come shopping with us," said Kelly her face brightening. "We'll have fun together."

Fran stared at her friend. "I don't want to go shopping. It's a stupid thing to do. Everything's stupid!" With those words Fran turned and started to run towards home.

Kelly watched until her friend was out of sight. Then she turned and walked slowly back to school.

Activity Sheet

1. Stress is tension, pressure, or strain that affects the mind and body. In the story "Let's Go Shopping," what was the stress in Fran's life? _____

2. Below is a list of ways some people behave when they feel stress. Circle the behaviors that you saw in Fran.

Get angry	Eat more than usual
Stop seeing friends	Stop usual activities
Increase activity	Appear sad/cry
Bite fingernails	Change moods frequently
Sleep more than usual	Stop eating
Sleep less than usual	Keep thinking about things over and over

3. Below are some suggestions of ways to help your mind and body when you are feeling stress. Add your suggestions in the blanks.

Take a walk	Talk with a friend	Do something relaxing
Breathe slowly	Imagine good things	Take a shower
_____	_____	_____

4. Kelly wanted to help her friend. What ways did she try to help?

_____

_____

If you had been Kelly, what would you have done? Suggest ways Kelly could help her friend in this time of stress.

_____

_____

_____

_____

_____

Let's Go Shopping
Stress Survey

Talk with other students about stress. Be certain they know what you are talking about when you use the word *stress*. Before doing your survey, answer the questions yourself. You are student #1.

1. First, ask them what causes stress in their lives. What has caused stress over the past few months? List their responses.
2. Next, talk about ways they have learned to deal with stress in their lives. List their suggested "stress-busters."

	Causes of Stress	Stress-Busters
Student #1 (me)		
Student #2		
Student #3		

Thinking It Over

Read the following situations and answer the questions.

1. Dave's coach just pulled Dave out of the game because he cannot concentrate. All he can think about is his dog Patches who has been hit by a car. The vet does not know whether Patches will live or not.

   How is Dave showing stress? _____

   How can Dave reduce his stress? _____

   _____

2. Ginny's cousin is getting married and Ginny has been asked to be in the wedding party. She has her dress and shoes and is very excited. On the morning of the wedding she wakes up with a splitting headache.

   How is Ginny showing stress? _____

   How can Ginny reduce her stress? _____

3. Tom usually likes to spend time with his younger brother Barry. But when Barry comes to play this evening Tom yells at him, "Can't you see I'm busy? I've got homework to do and this science project is due tomorrow!" Barry leaves in tears.

   How is Tom showing stress? _____

   How can Tom reduce his stress? _____

   _____

4. Tell about a time you experienced stress. _____

   _____

   _____

   _____

   How did your stress show? _____

   What could you have done to reduce your stress? _____

The Date

Overview

Rules and regulations are part of our lives. But there is continual tension as individuals grow and change and find rules too restrictive. Christy wants to date but the rule in her house forbids her dating until she is 15.

Objectives

1. Identify behaviors people may use to "bend" a rule and possible responses when they fail.
2. List household rules.
3. Practice the skill of negotiating.

Preparation

Make one copy of each of the following pages of "The Date" for each student:

You Decide   Household Rules

Activity Sheet   Thinking It Over

Presentation

Talk with students about rules at their homes. Do they have any rules about dating? Explain that this dialogue centers on a disagreement about dating between Christy and her mother. Distribute copies of "You Decide." Have students read the story.

Distribute copies of "Activity Sheet." Students may work with a partner to answer the questions and write Part II of the story. (If students have an alternate response to the three listed, they can use it in their writing.) Have students share their writing with their classmates.

Expand the discussion about household rules. In addition to dating, what other issues are covered in household rules? Distribute copies of "Household Rules." Allow students time to write their rules on the paper.

Talk with students about negotiating. What is it? When is it appropriate? How does one go about negotiating? Have students work with a partner to do #2 and #3 on the activity sheet, which will give them an opportunity to role-play some negotiating. Each pair will do two role-plays with each one taking a turn as himself or herself trying to negotiate a change and a turn as the partner's parent.

Distribute copies of "Thinking It Over." Have students answer the questions.

You Decide

"Good-night. I'm going up to bed." Christy gave her mother a kiss on the cheek.

Christy's mother was paying bills and had papers spread all over the kitchen table. "Good-night honey. Sleep well." She didn't even look up from the check she was writing.

Christy headed for the hall. "Oh, by the way—I won't be home tomorrow evening," said Christy.

"You won't? What are you doing?"

"Going out," replied Christy casually.

"Going out where?" Her mother stopped writing and looked at Christy. "With whom?"

"Just going to a movie," Christy said lightly. "I'm really tired so I'm going to bed now."

"You didn't answer my question," said her mother putting her pen down.

"What question was that?" Christy tried to stall.

"Who are you going to a movie with?"

Christy could tell her mother was going to insist on an answer. "Oh it's somebody I sort of know from school."

"Who exactly?"

"You know Jessica? She's one of the kids I do stuff with—and Mia and B. J. and Cindy."

"So you're all going to the movies?" Christy's mother was puzzled. Christy frequently did things with a group of friends from school. Why was she being so evasive?

"Well not exactly," admitted Christy.

"Who exactly?"

"Well, it's Jessica's brother."

"He's going with the rest of you?"

"Well, not exactly."

"Then what? EXACTLY!" Christy's mother was beginning to get impatient.

"Jessica said he wants to go out with just me."

"No. Absolutely not!" Christy's mother was firm. "You know the rule. No dating until you are 15!"

"But, Mom, please! Can I please go? Everybody else is dating."

"I sincerely doubt that is true, Christy. Does Jessica's brother go to your school? Why don't you invite him to join you and your friends and you all go to a movie?"

"He wouldn't want to hang out with us."

"Why not?"

"He's in high school."

"How old is he?"

"He's 16 but he's really nice and . . . ."

"The subject is closed. You are not going to the movies with Jessica's brother tomorrow night. Do you understand?"

"I knew you'd say that," Christy's voice began to rise. "You always treat me like a baby. I never get to do anything fun."

Christy ran up the stairs and stormed off to her room.

Activity Sheet

1. In the story, "The Date," Christy tries several ways to get what she wants. Give an example of each method.

   Being Sneaky:_____

   Pleading: _____

   Anger: _____

2. Christy's mother has said "No." Christy now has several ways she can respond. Tell what her actions might be for each choice.

   Sulking: _____

   Sneaking: _____

   Accepting: _____

3. Choose one response in #2. With a partner, write Part II of the story. If Christy decides to respond in this way, what might she do? (You may write on the back of this paper.)

_____

_____

_____

_____

_____

_____

_____

_____

_____

_____

Household Rules

1. One rule in Christy's house is that you have to be at least 15 to date. What are some of the rules in your home? List at least five of these rules.

HOUSEHOLD RULES

a. _____
_____

b. _____
_____

c. _____
_____

d. _____
_____

e. _____
_____

2. Choose one rule you would like to see changed. (If there isn't one, assume you are Christy and want the age-of-dating rule changed.) One method for creating change is to *negotiate*. With a friend acting as your parent, try to negotiate a change in this rule. What change do you want? Why is your change better than the original rule? What are you willing to give up to get what you want?

Two cautions if you are trying to negotiate a change:
1. Be selective about the time and setting you choose for negotiations.
2. Be prepared that it may be a nonnegotiable matter. The other person may be unwilling to make a change.

Thinking It Over

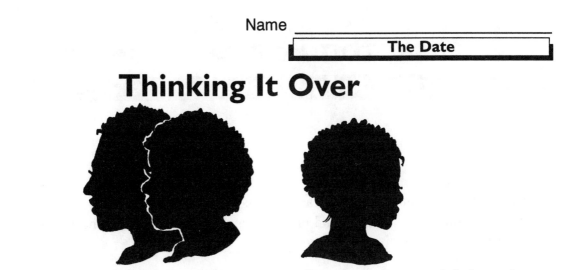

1. In the story, "The Date," Christy's mother was very firm about the age-of-dating rule. What might be some of the reasons she thought her middle-school daughter was too young to date? _____

_____

Do you agree or disagree? Why? _____

_____

_____

2. Think about a time you and your parent(s) disagreed about something you wanted to do. What was the situation? What happened? Why did your parent(s) take that particular position?

_____

_____

_____

_____

_____

If you were in the same situation again, what would you do or say differently?

_____

_____

_____

_____

_____

_____

_____

_____

Basketball or Baby-sitting?

TEACHER INFORMATION

Overview

As pre-adolescents become more involved in school and a world outside their homes, it is natural for there to be conflicts between the needs of the family and the needs of the student. Josh is a good student and an important member of his school basketball team. But the family is feeling some financial pressure, and Josh is needed at home to care for his younger brother while his mother works.

Objectives

1. Explore conflicts between family needs and the desires of the student.
2. Gather information to make a wise decision.
3. Consider compromise solutions to an either-or situation.

Preparation

Make one copy of each of the following pages of "Basketball or Baby-sitting?" for each student:

You Decide   Thinking It Over

Make one copy of each of the following pages:

Witness: Josh's mother, Mrs. Evans   Witness: Josh's father, Mr. Evans
Witness: Josh's little brother, Toby   Witness: Josh
Witness: Josh's friend, Scott   Witness: Josh's coach, Mr. Nyland
Presenter: Josh should baby-sit for his brother   Presenter: Josh should play basketball

Make one copy for each remaining student (total in the class minus 8):

Observer: Basketball or Baby-sitting?

Presentation

Day 1

Talk with students about conflict. Do they ever have a conflict between something their family expects them to do and something they would rather do with their friends?

Distribute copies of "You Decide." Have students read the story. Discuss the two choices Josh has. Take a vote. How many think Josh should play basketball? How many think Josh should baby-sit for his little brother?

Use a "courtroom" to gather more information about Josh's situation. Talk with students about courtroom dramas they may have seen on television. How does a courtroom operate?

Select a student to present each case. (You may choose to have an assistant for each presenter.) Select six students to take the parts of the witnesses. Give students copies of the page that tells about the role they will be playing in the courtroom. Reading the information and answering the questions will help them develop their characters.

Have the presenter for the "Baby-sitting Case" meet with Mrs. Evans, Mr. Evans, and Toby to plan their strategy. The presenter for the "Basketball Case" meets with Josh, Scott, and Mr. Nyland to plan their strategy. Students will complete their preparations as homework.

Talk with the remaining students about their roles in the drama. They will be *mediators*. Discuss the meaning of the word. Their job will be to hear the information presented and to try to find a solution that will satisfy both sides. Distribute copies of "Observer: Basketball or Baby-sitting?" for students to complete as they listen to each witness.

Day 2
Arrange the classroom to resemble a courtroom. Place a witness chair in the front of the room. Have a desk for each of the presenters.

Serve as the judge, maintaining order and keeping things moving. Decide which case will present first (perhaps by flipping a coin). The presenter calls each witness and asks questions. The opposing presenter cross-examines each witness.

The opposing case is presented.

The observers are given an opportunity to ask questions of the witnesses for information not already brought forth.

The observers suggest alternate solutions. Write each solution on the board as it is given. Talk about the suggested alternatives. Who would be affected by each choice? How would Mr. and Mrs. Evans and other people feel about each of these options?

Distribute copies of "Thinking It Over." Have students answer the questions. Discuss them as time allows.

You Decide

The door slammed shut behind Josh and his friend, Scott, as they entered the kitchen. "Hi Mom! What's for supper?" inquired Josh as he lifted the cover off the kettle on the stove. "Hmmmm . . . smells good. Can Scott stay for supper?" Scott pulled a chair out from the kitchen table and sat down. Josh went to the refrigerator. "Is there anything to eat now?"

"Dinner will be ready in just a few minutes . . . don't you think you can wait?" Mrs. Evans smiled slightly as she watched her older boy. Josh was a fine son—so handsome and athletic and a fine student. He'd never given his parents any reason to worry. He loved sports, especially basketball, and was expected to be chosen as a starter for his school team again this year.

She hated to ask him what she and her husband had agreed to ask him tonight. But there seemed to be no other way. "It's not a very good night for Scott to stay," she answered Josh. "We need to talk about some things."

"Like what?" Josh closed the refrigerator door and turned to his mother. "What's up?"

"It's about the job I applied for. I heard from them yesterday."

"Did you get the job?" asked Josh.

"Yes, they hired me."

"You'll do great, Mom!"

"There's something more. I had hoped to work the early shift and be home when Toby gets home from school. But there are no openings. I have to work second shift. So I will work from three o'clock in the afternoon until eleven o'clock at night."

"So . . . that's cool!"

"Well, it's not quite that simple. I won't be home when your brother gets home from school. And someone needs to be here with him."

"He'll be OK," said Josh.

"No, he's too young to be left alone. He's only in first grade. Seven years old is too young to be alone at home for the afternoon."

"So who will watch him?" asked Josh.

"It'll have to be you," responded his mother. Your father and I want to talk with you about this tonight. I can't think of anyone else to watch Toby."

"Me?!" exclaimed Josh. A look of disbelief crossed his face.

"Josh can't do it either, Mrs. Evans," said Scott. "We've got basketball practice every day after school. It lasts until 5:30."

"I'm so sorry about this," said Mrs. Evans, reaching out to lay her hand on Josh's shoulder. "I know how important basketball is to you and I want you to play. But there's no other way. We need you to watch Toby."

"I won't do it! I have to play basketball."

"The team needs him, Mrs. Evans," said Scott. "He's the best player on the team. He's got to play. It's important for the whole school."

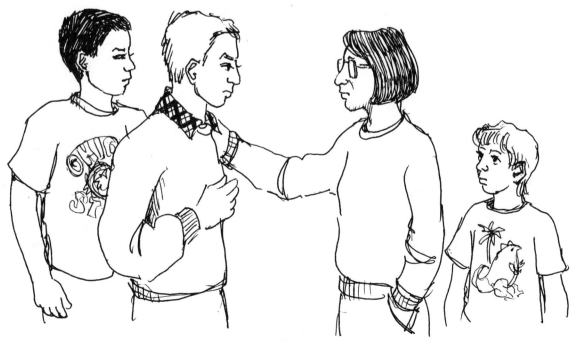

Witness: Josh's Mother, Mrs. Evans

Read the following information about Josh's mother and then answer the questions as you prepare to play the role of Mrs. Evans. Try to think how a mother would reason and feel.

Mrs. Evans is devoted to her family. She stopped working in a local bank two weeks before Josh was born and has not worked outside her home for over 14 years. Much has changed in the business world during that time. Mrs. Evans does not know how to use a computer and does not have other skills needed in the work force today. So she feels quite fortunate to have been hired at this mail-order house. They will train her to use a computer, and Mrs. Evans is hoping she will be able to get a job with better hours when she has these skills.

With Toby in school all day, Mrs. Evans thought she could go back to work and help with the family finances. Her plan did not include working second shift. Mrs. Evans hates to ask Josh to watch Toby, but Toby loves Josh and someone has to be with him. He's just too young to be alone with all the strange things that happen these days. She thought of asking her sister, but she is having marriage problems, and it did not seem to be a good idea.

Basketball is so important to Josh, and he will hate to give up the team. But it will be just as important to him next year when he is in high school. And maybe if Mrs. Evans gets some training now, she will be able to get a job with better hours which will allow Josh to play sports.

1. What are the reasons you are taking the job at the mail-order house?

_____

_____

2. Why are you asking Josh to watch Toby after school?

_____

_____

3. Are you a "good" mother? Why or why not?

_____

_____

Witness: Josh's Father, Mr. Evans

Read the following information about Josh's father and then answer the questions as you prepare to play the role of Mr. Evans. Try to think how a father would reason and feel.

Mr. Evans has worked for 15 years at the manufacturing plant in town. He has a good job and gets a regular paycheck, but it never seems to be quite enough. He manages to pay the rent and put food on the table for his family, but there is no money for extras.

Lately there have been many extra medical bills. Josh and Toby's grandmother lived with the Evans family for almost two years before she died last spring. She was quite ill and there are still many hospital and doctor bills needing to be paid.

Mr. Evans does not want his wife to work, but it seems to be a necessity. They have got to be planning ahead. Josh will be ready for college in just a few years. Neither of them was able to attend college, but both Mr. and Mrs. Evans are hoping Josh will go. They know it will be expensive and they need to start saving now.

Mr. Evans is proud of his son's skills as a basketball player. He's sorry that Josh will have to quit basketball, but somebody has to watch Toby. School and basketball are all well and good, but a family has to stick together. There's just no other way.

1. Why do you think your wife should go to work?

   _____

   _____

2. Why are you asking Josh to watch Toby after school?

   _____

   _____

3. Are you a "good" father? Why or why not?

   _____

   _____

Witness: Josh's Little Brother, Toby

Read the following information about Toby and then answer the questions as you prepare to play the role of Toby. Remember that Toby is only seven. Try to think the way a seven-year-old would reason and feel.

Toby is seven and in the first grade at school. After school, he always comes straight home on the bus. His mother fixes him a snack and they talk about what happened at school. Then, sometimes his mother lets him play with his friend, Rico, who lives in the next block. Or he watches TV or plays with the dog. Sometimes Rico comes to his house.

But Toby's favorite thing to do after school is to be with his brother, Josh. He has fun with Josh and likes it when they throw a basketball back and forth. Sometimes Josh takes him to the park when he is shooting hoops. If there are other guys there from Josh's school, they like to play a game of basketball. Toby is too little to play, but he watches and sometimes runs after the ball when it goes out of bounds. After they finish playing, Josh and his friends take turns lifting Toby up on their shoulders so he can put the ball through the hoop.

Josh is not home in the afternoon much these days. He has basketball practice after school, so Toby does not usually see him until suppertime.

1. How do you you feel about your mother going to work?

_____

_____

2. When your mother starts working, she wants Josh to be home when you get home from school. What do you think about that idea?

_____

_____

3. What do you think Josh wants to do? What makes you think this?

_____

_____

Witness: Josh

Read the following information about Josh and then answer the questions as you prepare to play the role of Josh.

Josh is 13 and he cannot remember when he did not love to play basketball. Before he was old enough for school, someone gave him a toy hoop and basketball which he played with for hours. Starting in the fourth grade, he played on the town's pee-wee basketball team. He's played on a team every year since and is a starter on the school team. Basketball is the most important thing in Josh's life.

Of course, his family is important too. Josh gets along well with both his parents. He knows his father works hard—and it was tough for his mother having to take care of his grandmother. Josh really likes his little brother, too. Some kids complain about having a younger sister or brother, but Josh thinks Toby is pretty special. He likes throwing the basketball with him and does not mind him hanging around when Josh is playing with his friends.

Although Josh likes his brother, he does not think it is fair that he may have to give up basketball to watch him after school. Basketball is too important. He knows his parents want him to go to college, and Josh is thinking he might be able to get a basketball scholarship. His coach says he's pretty good. But he needs to keep playing and working. Josh's dream is to play professional basketball.

1. How do you feel about your mother going to work?

   _____

   _____

2. How do you contribute to your family?

   _____

   _____

3. Why do you think you should be allowed to play basketball instead of watching your brother after school?

   _____

   _____

Witness: Josh's Friend, Scott

Read the following information about Scott and then answer the questions as you prepare to play the role of Scott.

Josh and Scott have been friends since the fourth grade. They played on the same pee-wee basketball team, and they have been playing basketball ever since. The two boys go to the park to shoot baskets no matter what the weather.

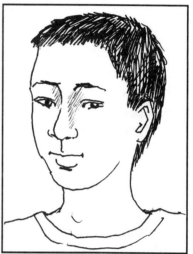

Scott's family lives in a home they own across town from the Evans family. Both his parents work. He has a younger sister and an older brother. When they were too young to be alone after school, his parents hired a woman to take care of them. She lived with them and was always there to watch the children when their parents were at work or out with friends.

Scott likes to go to Josh's house. Mrs. Evans is a pretty nice lady. She laughs a lot and she likes to make cookies. Even when their grandmother was there and pretty sick, Mrs. Evans liked to have Scott come to the house. Mr. Evans seems OK too, although he works long hours and Scott does not see him very often.

As little brothers go, Toby is a good kid. But Scott does not think he should be Josh's responsibility. Josh needs to play basketball. Scott and the team and the whole school are counting on him.

1. How is Josh's family different from your family?

   _____

   _____

2. Why do you think Josh's parents want him to watch Toby?

   _____

   _____

3. Why do you think Josh should be allowed to play basketball?

   _____

   _____

Name _____

Read the following information about Josh's coach and then answer the questions as you prepare to play the role of Mr. Nyland. Try to think how a coach would reason and feel.

Mr. Nyland has been teaching gym and coaching basketball for 18 years, 10 of them at this school. Josh is one of the best players he has ever coached. Josh has athletic ability, and he also works hard. With Josh's contributions, this year's team may be the best one his school has ever had. Mr. Nyland is thinking it may be a championship team and is wondering if this is the year they will bring the trophy home.

Mr. Nyland does not want to lose Josh from the team—and it is not just for the sake of the team. He is also thinking of Josh. If he keeps working hard and developing, Mr. Nyland thinks Josh could get a basketball scholarship to college. He knows the Evans family does not have much money, and a basketball scholarship could be Josh's ticket to college.

But every year of playing is important. If he is going to be a star, Josh has got to keep playing right now. Mr. Nyland has seen this kind of thing happen before. A player has potential and then something interferes. There is family pressure, or some other interest takes attention away from basketball. That should not happen to Josh. Josh needs to practice and play with the team. Maybe he could go to basketball camp this summer. It is important for Josh's future.

1. How will you benefit if Josh is allowed to play basketball?

   _____

   _____

2. Why do you think Josh should be allowed to play basketball?

   _____

   _____

3. What do you think will happen if Josh takes a year off from playing basketball for his school team?

   _____

   _____

Presenter: Josh should baby-sit for his brother

1. What are the reasons this is the choice Josh should make? _____

   _____

   _____

2. The witnesses for your case will be Mrs. Evans, Mr. Evans, and Toby. What questions will you ask each witness to get information to support your case?

Witness	Questions
Mrs. Evans	
Mr. Evans	
Toby	

3. The other presenter will call Josh, Scott, and Mr. Nyland as witnesses. What questions will you ask them?

Witness	Questions
Josh	
Scott	
Mr. Nyland	

4. Prepare an opening statement. In a few sentences, tell the observers what they will learn as they listen to the witnesses. Use the back of this paper to write your statement.

Presenter: Josh should play basketball

1. What are the reasons this is the choice Josh should make?

   _____

   _____

2. The witnesses for your case will be Josh, Scott, and Mr. Nyland. What questions will you ask each witness to get information to support your case?

Witness	Questions
Josh	
Scott	
Mr. Nyland	

3. The other presenter will call Mrs. Evans, Mr. Evans, and Toby as witnesses. What questions will you ask them?

Witness	Questions
Mrs. Evans	
Mr. Evans	
Toby	

4. Prepare an opening statement. In a few sentences, tell the observers what they will learn as they listen to the witnesses. Use the back of this paper to write your statement.

Observer: Basketball or Baby-sitting?

1. Listen carefully to each witness. What information do you learn from each witness that will help you in making a decision?

Witness	Information Learned from This Witness
Josh	
Mrs. Evans	
Mr. Evans	
Toby	
Scott	
Mr. Nyland	

2. Two cases have been presented. Either Josh plays basketball or he stays home to watch his brother. In either case, someone wins and someone loses. Think about the information you heard. What other possible solutions can you suggest?

_____

_____

Thinking It Over

1. When you first read the story about Josh, what choice did you think he should make?

   _____

2. After listening to the case being presented for each side and considering alternatives, what do you think would be the best choice for Josh? _____

   _____

3. Did your choice change? Why or why not? _____

4. Josh faced a choice between the needs of his family and something important to him outside the family. Think about a movie or TV character you have seen who had to make that same kind of choice. What did the character's family (parents) want?

   _____

5. What did the character want to do outside the family? _____

   _____

6. What choice did the character make? How was the choice made?

   _____

7. In your opinion, was this a good choice? Why or why not?

   _____

8. Think about a time in your own life when you had to make a choice between the desires of your family and something important to you. What was the situation?

   _____

9. What choice did you make? _____

   How did you go about making your choice? _____

   _____

10. If faced with that situation today, how would you make a choice?

   _____

   _____

Chores to Do

Overview

In a family, everyone has a specific role. Children are frequently assigned chores as a way they can contribute and learn responsibility at the same time. Chores can also be the subject of squabbles between sisters and brothers. Kathy has done her work, but Doug is putting off his chores. Kathy does not think that is right.

Objectives

1. Explore sibling conflicts.
2. Identify possible choices and choices made in conflict situations.
3. List chores and responsibilities of each family member.

Preparation

Make one copy of each of the following pages of "Chores to Do" for each student:

You Decide

Activity Sheet

Family Chores and Responsibilities

Thinking It Over

Presentation

Talk with students about chores. Discuss who does what chores and their feelings about the way chores are handled in their families.

Distribute copies of "You Decide." Explain to the class that this story is about chores in a family and the conflict a brother and sister have had over their chores. Let students read the story.

Instruct the class not to think about who was right or wrong in the story, but to focus on Kathy and the possible choices she had and the choices she made. Distribute copies of "Activity Sheet." Talk with students about the flow chart and how it works. Have students work individually or in pairs to complete the flow chart of Kathy's choices and then to make a flow chart of Doug's choices.

Have students make a chart of chores that their own family members are assigned. Distribute copies of "Family Chores and Responsibilities." If any students in the class are without sisters and/or brothers, have them survey several classmates and compare the chores each is expected to do.

Distribute copies of "Thinking It Over." Have students answer the questions. Discuss their answers.

You Decide

"You're going to be in big trouble." Kathy stood in the doorway of the living room, hands on her hips. Her brother was sprawled on the sofa, watching TV. He ignored her, hoping she would just go away.

But Kathy had no intention of being ignored. She moved into the living room and continued talking to Doug. "You know Mom said we have to do our chores right after school. But you're just sitting here watching TV. She'll be pretty mad if they're not done when she gets home!"

"What?" asked Doug, looking up from the TV as a commercial came on. "What are you talking about? What chores?"

"You know very well what I'm talking about. You're supposed to vacuum the living room and take out the trash and put your clean clothes away in your room. It's not all that much to do, but you ought to do your share. Mom works hard and she shouldn't have to do all the housework too when she gets home."

"Yeah, I'll do it . . . . I'll get it done." ·

"Well, you better get started! It'll take time to do it right. You have to move the furniture and vacuum behind the chairs. You can't just run the vacuum through the middle of the room. And you need to empty the wastebaskets in all the rooms before you take out the trash. Mom will be home in less than an hour."

"Yeah, OK."

Neither Doug nor Kathy moved. "Well . . . when are you going to start?" Kathy asked her brother.

"Don't sweat it. I said I'll do it and I will. Nobody put you in charge of my life. You don't need to stand over me all the time."

"I'm not standing over you. I'm just trying to be sure you do your share. You're so lazy. You'd just lie on that couch and not lift a finger to help around here."

"Shhhh. I can't hear the TV with you yapping at me."

"I am not yapping. And you'd better get going or you won't get done in time and Mom'll kill us."

"If it's so important to you, why don't you vacuum and take out the trash? You're standing around with nothing to do but yell at me. I'm busy."

"But I already did my share of the chores. I washed the dishes and swept the kitchen floor and did the laundry. It's not fair if I have to do all the work around here and you get away without doing anything. Besides, you're not busy. You're just watching TV like you always do. You should be doing your chores, not trying to get me to do them!"

"Well, you don't have to do them. But be quiet, will ya? I'm trying to watch this show. Stuff a sock in it."

"No, I won't. I don't want to hear Mom yell just because you're so lazy. Why won't you do your share of the work?"

"Tell you what: you do the chores and I'll pay you for my share."

"Oh no, I'm not falling for that again! Last time you said you'd pay me, and you never did. I'm not doing your chores so you can just sit around and watch TV! Get up and do them yourself!"

"Get lost, will you? I'm trying to watch this program."

Kathy went over to the TV and turned it off. "No, I won't get lost. You get up and get to work!"

Doug was mad. "Get out of here," he yelled. "What I do is none of your business." He got up off the couch and headed for his sister. "Turn that TV back on, or you will be sorry!"

Activity Sheet

In the story, "Chores to Do," Kathy makes several choices about what she will do. Complete the flow chart to show the possible choices Kathy had and the choices she made.

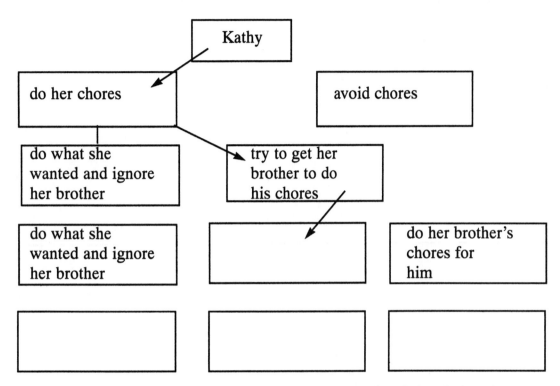

Make a flow chart below that shows the possible choices Doug had and the choices he made.

Chores to Do
Family Chores and Responsibilities

What chores and responsibilities do you have in your family? What are the chores and
responsibilities of other members of your family? Complete the following chart.

People in Family	Daily Chores	Weekly Chores

Are the chores in your family fairly divided? _____ Explain your answer. What
changes would you make if you could?

_____

_____

_____

Thinking It Over

1. In the story, "Chores to Do," who is older: Doug or Kathy? _____
   Explain your answer.

   _____

   _____

   _____

2. Think about a conflict you have had in your family—with a sister or brother, parent,
   cousin, or some other person. Describe the situation.

   _____

   _____

   _____

3. Make a flow chart that shows the possible choices you had and the choices you made in
   the situation described above.

4. If you were in the situation again, what choices could you make differently?

   _____

   _____

The Surprise Package

TEACHER INFORMATION

Overview

Split families are a fact of our culture. The resulting relationships that middle school students have with their biological parents can be tangled and filled with complicated emotions. Mya lives with her mother and has not heard from her father since she was a baby. She receives a package from her father filled with birthday presents.

Objectives

1. Identify a wide range of emotions and feelings.
2. Recognize words and behaviors that indicate a specific feeling.

Preparation

Make one copy of each of the following pages of "The Surprise Package" for each student:

You Decide	Feeling Faces
Activity Sheet	Thinking It Over

Presentation

Talk with students about feelings. What are different feelings they have? What kinds of things make them feel one way or another?

Distribute copies of "Feeling Faces." What feelings are listed that students already identified? What new feelings are shown that have not been talked about?

There are two blank faces at the bottom of the page. Ask students to be thinking of other feelings and faces they could show to illustrate those feelings.

Distribute copies of "You Decide." Ask students to read the story and think about the feelings Mya had in this situation.

After students finish reading the story, distribute copies of "Activity Sheet." Students may choose feelings and faces from the "Feeling Faces" page or identify and illustrate other feelings. Sometimes a line from the story may indicate more than one feeling.

Discuss "Activity Sheet" with the class. What feelings did they identify in the story? What additional sentences did the students choose?

Distribute copies of "Thinking It Over." Have students answer the questions.

You Decide

[*A knock is heard at the door.*]

"I'll get it!" Mya ran and opened the front door.

"Package for Mya Leighton," announced the delivery man standing on the porch.

"That's me!"

"Sign here," said the delivery man. "This is a pretty big package. Somebody must think you are very special!"

Mya signed her name on the clipboard. "Thanks," she said, and balancing the package in both arms, she went back into the living room.

"Who was at the door?" asked her mother as she came down the stairs.

"A delivery man brought a package. It's for me!" Mya placed the box on the floor, knelt down beside it, and began ripping off the paper. "I wonder who sent this."

"Maybe it's a birthday present," suggested her mother.

"Yeah, I figured that out—my birthday is the day after tomorrow. But *who* is sending me a present?"

"Keep opening, and we'll soon know."

Mya finished removing the brown paper and opened the box. "It's not just *one* present!" she exclaimed. "It's a whole box of presents." One by one she lifted out the brightly wrapped gifts. Several looked as though they might contain clothes—perhaps a sweater or a blouse. One small box resembled a jewelry case. There were others that Mya couldn't even guess what they contained.

"But who are they from?" Mya kept lifting out packages. "Here's a card," she said, reaching the bottom of the box. "That'll tell." Eagerly she tore open the envelope.

As she read the note on the card, a cloud passed across Mya's face. "Oh," she said as she backed away from the box and sat down on the floor. "Why did they have to be from him? Now my birthday is ruined!"

"What's wrong?" asked her mother. "Who sent you the gifts?"

Mya said nothing, but handed her mother the card. "Oh . . . they're from your father." Mya's parents had divorced when she was just a baby. Her father lived several hundred miles away and had no contact with them at all.

"Why did he have to go and do this?" asked Mya. "He never sent me any birthday presents before. I never got a present at Christmas from him or even a card. Why is he doing this now?"

"I don't know, honey."

"He's always too busy with those other girls!" Mya's father had remarried and had two daughters with his second wife. "I bet he gives them presents and does things with them all the time. I bet he never missed *their* birthdays."

"In his card, your father says that he's sorry about missing all these years with you," said her mother. "I guess that's what he's trying to say by sending you all these presents."

"Well, I don't want them. He can have them back." Mya began throwing the packages back in the box. "I don't care if I ever see or hear from him again in my whole life!"

"You don't mean that," said her mother. "You used to ask me about your father all the time and you wished he would come and do things with you like other girls' fathers do."

"That's what I used to say," agreed Mya. "That was when I was little. But he never came. And now I don't want to see him, and I don't want anything from him."

"These are lovely gifts," said Mya's mother. "Maybe you'd like to open them and see if they are things you like."

"No, I don't want anything from him," Mya said again. "He's *not* my father."

Activity Sheet

1. In the story, "The Surprise Package," Mya had several different feelings. Read the sentences below. What emotion does it show? Draw a "face" that shows her feelings beside each sentence.

"A delivery man brought a package. It's for me!" Mya placed the box on the floor, knelt down beside it, and began ripping off the paper.

_____

"It's not just *one* present!" she exclaimed. "It's a whole box of presents."

_____

As she read the card, a cloud passed across Mya's face. "Oh," she said as she backed away from the box and sat down on the floor.

_____

2. Choose two more sentences from the story that show Mya's feelings. Write each sentence below. Draw a face beside each sentence.

Name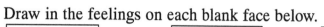

The Surprise Package
Feeling Faces

Draw in the feelings on each blank face below.

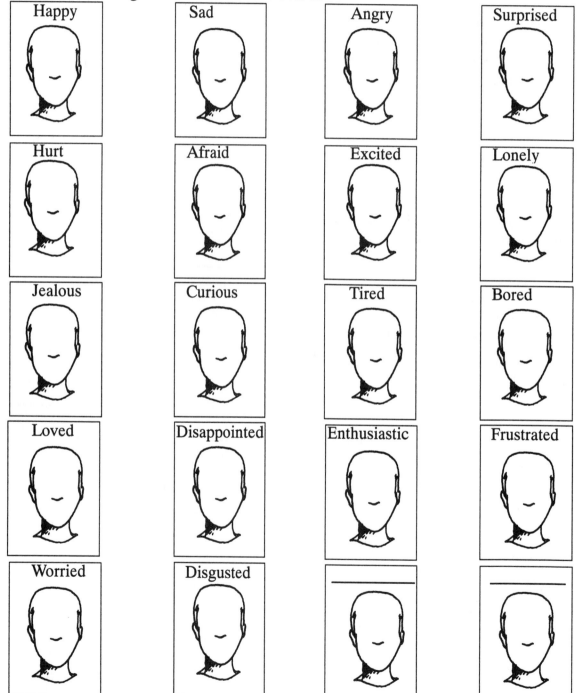

Happy	Sad	Angry	Surprised
Hurt	Afraid	Excited	Lonely
Jealous	Curious	Tired	Bored
Loved	Disappointed	Enthusiastic	Frustrated
Worried	Disgusted		

Name _____

Thinking It Over

1. In the story, "The Surprise Package," Mya did not want to keep the birthday presents from her father. What feelings about her father helped her make that decision?

   _____

2. What would you have done if you were Mya and received the surprise package? Explain your answer. _____

   _____

3. Think about a situation in which you have had a lot of conflicting feelings at the same time. Is there a time when somebody got something that you wanted? Or when you were not included in an outing? Tell what happened. Beside each sentence, write a word or two that tells how you were feeling.

What Happened	**Feelings**
_____	_____
_____	_____
_____	_____
_____	_____
_____	_____
_____	_____

What choice did you make about what to do? _____

_____

Staying with Mom

TEACHER INFORMATION

Overview

Alcohol abuse affects many families. In some, the alcoholic becomes loud, aggressive, and mean. In other situations, the pain and suffering inflicted on the family is more subtle. Steve lives with his mother who goes on periodic drinking binges. He never knows when he will come home to find her depending on him.

Objectives

1. Identify some ways an alcoholic can affect other family members.
2. Examine steps in the 12-step program.
3. Find ways some of the Alateen slogans apply to everyday life.

Preparation

Make one copy of each of the following pages of "Staying with Mom" for each student:

    You Decide   Understanding the 12 Steps
    Activity Sheet   Thinking It Over
    The 12 Steps

Have dictionaries available for students to use.

Presentation

Talk with students about alcoholism. How does an alcoholic behave? How does an alcoholic's behavior affect other members of the family?

Distribute copies of "You Decide." Have students read the story, noticing how Steve is thinking and behaving in the situation.

Talk with students about Steve's actions. Why does he make the choices he does? Distribute copies of "Activity Sheet" for students to complete.

One group that helps alcoholics is Alcoholics Anonymous (AA). Talk with students about Alateen, which is one of the Al-Anon Family Groups that helps young people whose lives are affected by alcohol. (Perhaps you can find someone to talk to the class about Alateen and how the program has helped them. However, this may not be possible because of the anonymity inherent in the program.) Distribute copies of "The 12 Steps." Have students read through the steps.

Distribute copies of "Understanding the 12 Steps." Students will work in pairs to match one of these statements with each of the original 12 steps.

AA programs have developed a number of slogans which offer good guidelines for everyone to live by. Distribute copies of "Thinking It Over." Discuss students' responses.

You Decide

"Steve, Steeeeeeeeeeeeve."

Steve was in his bedroom listening to music. He turned up the volume and tried not to hear the voice calling his name.

"St-e-e-e-e-e-eve, I need you."

His mother's voice could not be ignored—Steve knew that from long experience. Reluctantly, he took off his earphones, got up off the bed, and headed toward the living room.

"Yeah, Mom . . . what do you want this time?"

His mother looked up from the couch where she was lying down. An empty liquor bottle was on the table by the sofa. "I thought you were here, but you took so long to come."

"I was in my room. But I'm here now. What do you want?"

"Come help me up. I need to go to the bathroom. I'm just a little shaky and I need some help. I'm afraid I might fall by myself."

"OK, just sit up first." His mother slowly shifted to a sitting position, with both feet on the floor. She leaned back against the couch to catch her breath.

"Let's get up now." Steve watched as his mother struggled to stand and then leaned against him as they walked toward the bathroom. Steve waited while she used the toilet and then helped her back to the couch.

"You're such a good son," said his mother. "I don't know how I'd ever manage without you, especially since your father moved out."

"Yeah," agreed Steve, envying his father. He wished he could move out too. But then what would his mother do? When she was on a drinking binge, she couldn't take care of herself—couldn't even get to the bathroom by herself.

"You wouldn't leave me, too? Would you, Steevie?" asked his mother as she lay down.

"Are you OK now?" asked Steve, pulling the afghan over his mother's shoulders. His father wanted Steve to come live with him. Steve thought about it often, but he didn't know what his mother would do without someone in the house. So he stayed with her.

"Z-Z-Z-Z" was the only reply. Steve watched his mother sleeping. "She must have been drinking the whole day while I was in school," he thought to himself. She'd been doing well—there had been several good weeks. He never knew when another round of drinking would start or what would set it off. Steve went back to his room, sat down at his desk, and began to do his math homework.

Steve was only on the second problem when the phone rang. He ran to get it, hoping the noise would not awaken his mother. "Hello," he said into the receiver.

"Hello, Steve. This is Mrs. Judkins. How are you today?"

"All right," answered Steve. Mary Judkins was a friend of his mother. In the days before his mother started drinking, they used to do a lot of things together.

"That's good to hear, Steve. Listen, I'm calling to talk to your mother. Is she there?"

"No, she's out," Steve lied to Mrs. Judkins. "I don't know when she'll be back."

"I'm sorry I missed her. Have her give me a call this evening, will you please?"

"Yeah, OK, if she can . . . good-bye."

"Good-bye," said Mrs. Judkins.

Steve hung up the phone. From the living room, he could hear his mother, "Steve. Steeeeve. Come get me a drink of water. My throat is so dry."

Activity Sheet

1. What sentences in "You Decide" make you think Steve feels resentful of his situation?

_____

_____

Why is Steve resentful? _____

_____

2. What sentences in the story make you think Steve tells lies in his situation?

_____

_____

Why does Steve tell lies? _____

_____

3. What sentences in the story make you think Steve feels guilty about his thoughts and feelings?

_____

_____

Why does Steve feel guilty?_____

_____

4. If you were Steve's friend, what would you advise him to do in his situation?

_____

_____

The 12 Steps

Alateen is a fellowship of young people whose lives have been affected by alcoholism in a family member or close friend. Participants help one another by sharing their experiences, their strength, and their hope. By applying the AA 12 steps to their lives, they grow mentally, emotionally, and spiritually.

The 12 steps are listed below. Read the steps with a friend. You may need to look up some words in a dictionary to understand their meanings.

As members of Alateen we . . .

1. Admitted we were powerless over alcohol—that our lives had become unmanageable.

2. Came to believe that a Power greater than ourselves could restore us to sanity.

3. Made a decision to turn our will and our lives over to the care of God as we understood Him.

4. Made a searching and fearless moral inventory of ourselves.

5. Admitted to God, to ourselves, and to another human being the exact nature of our wrongs.

6. Were entirely ready to have God remove all these defects of character.

7. Humbly asked Him to remove our shortcomings.

8. Made a list of all persons we had harmed and became willing to make amends to them all.

9. Made direct amends to such people wherever possible, except when to do so would injure them or others.

10. Continued to take personal inventory and when we were wrong, promptly admitted it.

11. Sought through prayer and meditation to improve our conscious contact with God as we understood Him, praying only for knowledge of His will for us and the power to carry that out.

12. Having had a spiritual awakening as the result of these steps, we tried to carry this message to others, and to practice these principles in all our affairs.

Understanding the 12 Steps

The statements below are simpler explanations of the 12 steps. Match each statement with one of the steps. Place the number of the step on the line before each statement.

_____ We are ready to change.

_____ We think about each day and our lives and our responsibilities for that day.

_____ We regularly remember the good we have done and admit when we are wrong.

_____ We identify mistakes we have made and people we have hurt (including ourselves).

_____ We share with others our new way of life.

_____ We did not cause a person's drinking problem and we can't cure it.

_____ We admit things we have done wrong.

_____ We ask for help.

_____ We try to do our best each day and trust God with the rest.

_____ We make up for hurts we have caused if we can, except when it would hurt others.

_____ We make a list of our good qualities and our faults.

_____ We don't have all the answers, but there is a greater power that can help us think straight.

Thinking It Over

1. Even if there is not an alcoholic in your life, the Alateen slogans offer good advice for everyday living. In a few words, explain what each of these slogans means.

Easy Does It

_____

_____

_____

_____

One Day at a Time

_____

_____

_____

_____

Keep It Simple

_____

_____

_____

_____

Together We Can Make It

_____

_____

_____

_____

2. Choose one slogan listed above. How can you use the message of this slogan to help your life today?

_____

_____

_____

_____

_____

_____

Dealing with Dad

Overview

It is perfectly normal for adolescents to be embarrassed by their parents. But sometimes feelings grow and can become a major conflict when no one is able to recognize and take responsibility. Mr. Dann is an enthusiastic fan at his daughter's baseball games, but Jana thinks he is too enthusiastic and she is embarrassed.

Objectives

1. Compare generalizations and "I" statements.
2. Express thoughts and feelings in "I" statements.
3. Identify generalizations and "I" statements in personal conversation.

Preparation

Make one copy of each of the following pages of "Dealing with Dad" for each student:

You Decide	"I" Messages
Activity Sheet	Thinking It Over

Have available a chalkboard.

Presentation

Talk with students about times they have been embarrassed by their parents. What did the parents do? Why was it embarrassing? How did the student react?

Explain that today's story is about a girl who is embarrassed by her father. Distribute copies of "You Decide." Have students read the story.

Distribute copies of "Activity Sheet." Have students answer the questions. Talk with the class about the conversation between Jana and Mr. Dann. Who was honest with their feelings? When did they get honest? What was the atmosphere like when they became honest?

Write some generalizations (Blue is the prettiest color.) and some "I" statements (I like the color blue best of all.) on the board. Talk with students about the difference. Have a student write a generalization on the board. Let another student rewrite the generalization as an "I" statement. Distribute copies of "'I' Messages." Have students work in pairs to complete the activity.

Distribute copies of "Thinking It Over." The beginning of the story has been rewritten with Jana making an "I" statement. Have students complete the story and share their versions with the class. (Note: Using "I" statements does not necessarily ensure that the conversation will go well. It does mean that a person chooses to take responsibility for his or her own feelings and thoughts.) Have students keep a log of the generalizations and "I" statements they make throughout the day.

You Decide

"So when's your next game?" Mr. Dann asked as he dropped down on the couch beside his daughter.

Jana was concentrating on her book and barely acknowledged her father's presence.

"When does my little slugger play again?" Mr. Dann repeated his question.

Jana looked up. "Uhhh . . . I don't know . . . sometime," and she returned to her book.

"Well, I want to know," insisted her father. "How can I come and cheer for you if I don't know when the game is?"

"You don't have to come, Dad."

"Don't have to come! What are you talking about? I *want* to come! I want to be there! You don't think your old man would miss a chance to see you play, do you?"

"It's OK, Dad." Jana struggled to find the right words. "I know you have to work and everything . . . ."

"What do you mean 'OK'? I'm not going to let work keep me from coming to my daughter's baseball games. Haven't I been to every game so far this season?" Mr. Dann reached out and put his arm affectionately around Jana's shoulder, pulling her close to him.

"Yeah, Dad, you have."

"And I'm not going to stop now! It's just too important. I'm proud to be the father of the best player on the team."

"I know you're proud of me," said Jana, struggling to get free of her father's hold. "You've been to enough games, Dad."

"*Proud* of you—I guess I'm *proud*! I may not have any sons, but you play better than any boy on that team! And I want to see you play. So, tell me, when's the next game?"

Jana closed her book. "Dad, please don't come to the game." She did not look at her father.

"Don't come? What are you talking about?" Mr. Dann was surprised and hurt by his daughter's request. "Why wouldn't you want me to come? Most kids feel lucky when their parents take an interest in what they're doing. Why would you want me to stay away?"

"It's no big deal."

"Other parents come."

"Yeah, but it's not that important. You really don't have to come. Mom never comes and you don't have to come either. I won't mind."

"Your mother hates baseball. That's why she doesn't go to your games. She just doesn't understand the sport like I do. Of course I'll be there. I want to see you lead your team all the way to the state championship. I'll be right there in the stands with the other parents."

"But they don't yell and scream like you do!" Jana threw her book down on the floor and stood up. She looked straight at her father. "You're always shouting at the coach or giving me instructions or bragging about me to the other people sitting around you."

"I'm just . . . ."

"It's embarrassing, Dad!" Jana continued to shout at her father. "Everybody notices. The kids say you think you know more than the coach. They want to know why you aren't coaching if you know so much. But they don't mean it—they're just making fun of you. I hate it." Jana started to cry and ran out of the room.

"But I get excited when . . . ." Her father's voice trailed off as he watched Jana go.

Activity Sheet

1. In the first half of the story, "Dealing with Dad," what reasons did Jana give for not telling her father about the next baseball game?

   _____

   _____

2. How did Jana feel when her father came to the games?

   _____

   _____

3. By the end of the story, Jana told her father the real reason she did not want him to come. What was the reason?

   _____

   _____

4. In the first half of the story, what reasons did Mr. Dann give for wanting to come to Jana's baseball game?

   _____

   _____

5. How did Mr. Dann feel at the games?

   _____

   _____

6. What other reasons can you suggest why Mr. Dann might have wanted to go to Jana's games?

   _____

   _____

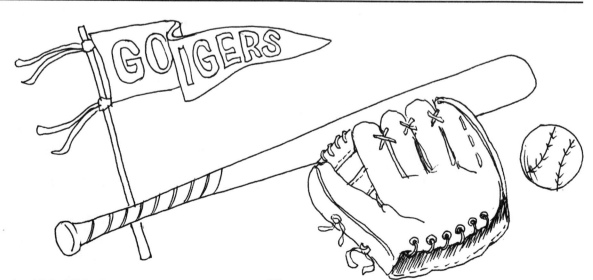

Dealing with Dad
"I" Messages

1. To live peacefully with others, people need to share what they are feeling and thinking. Learn to make "I" statements that tell what *you* think and feel. Look at the generalizations below. Then read the "I" statement beside each generalization.

Generalization	"I" Statement
Nobody likes broccoli.	I do not like broccoli.
My little sister is a pest.	I get annoyed at my little sister when she wants to play with me and my friends.
Everybody loves summer!	I think summer is the best season of the year.
Basketball is stupid.	I don't like to play basketball or watch others play it.

2. Read the generalizations below. Rewrite each one as an "I" statement.

Generalization	"I" Statement
Snow is wonderful!	_____
Everybody loves the book, *Black Beauty*.	_____
School is boring.	_____
His clothes are weird.	_____
Rock music is cool.	_____

3. Work with a partner. One person makes a generalization. The partner rewrites the generalization as an "I" statement. Use the back of this paper.

Thinking It Over

1. Here is a new start to the story, "Dealing with Dad." What might happen next? You write the rest of the story. Continue the story on the back of this paper.

    "So when's your next game?" Mr. Dann asked as he dropped down on the couch beside his daughter.

    Jana looked at her dad and then leaned over and gave him a kiss. "Dad, I've been wanting to talk to you about my baseball games. Sometimes I feel embarrassed when you yell during the games and I wish you weren't there."

2. Listen carefully to your conversations over the next 24 hours. When do you make generalizations? What "I" statements do you make? Keep a list.

Generalizations

_____
_____
_____
_____
_____

"I" Statements

_____
_____
_____
_____
_____

3. Restate your generalizations as "I" statements.

_____
_____
_____
_____
_____

The Chess Game

Overview

Pressure from friends can easily lead young people to do things they might have not even considered on their own. Pat and Jamie are good friends who often play chess together after school. Then one day, Pat wants to have a drink from the family liquor supply and tries to entice Jamie to come along.

Objectives

1. List potential responses to pressure from friends.
2. Identify situations where peer pressure influences decision-making.

Preparation

Make one copy for each student of the following:

     You Decide   Thinking It Over

Talk with students about peer pressure. What is it? When have students experienced peer pressure? When have they exerted peer pressure on others?

Distribute copies of "You Decide." This story is entirely dialogue. Read the story together. Have one student read the part of Pat and a second student read the part of Jamie. (These names were chosen so that both parts can be played by either boys or girls.) Ask students to think about what might happen next in this situation.

Divide the class into pairs. In each pair, one person will take the part of Jamie and the other will be Pat. They will read the dialogue together a second time and then write a continuation of the dialogue. What happens next? Use the back of the paper for writing this dialogue.

Presentation

As a class, discuss the various scenarios students have written. Which are believable? Which are responses students would be likely to make?

Distribute copies of "Thinking It Over." Ask students to respond to each situation and write their answers on the activity sheet. As students complete their individual work, they can discuss their answers with their partners. If there is time, conclude the class with a general discussion of how students responded to questions on the activity sheet.

You Decide

Jamie: "Hurry up . . . you're taking forever! I like playing chess with you, Pat. But sometimes you take so long deciding on a play! It's exasperating."

Pat: "I was just thinking . . . ."

Jamie: "I know you were, but don't take all day. I've got homework. You've got to pick up the pace if you want to finish this before I have to go."

Pat: "I wasn't thinking about chess . . . Jamie, we're the only ones in the house."

Jamie: "Of course we are. Your sister is working at the grocery store and your parents never get home from work until after six. What's the big deal?"

Pat: "I was thinking—we could have a drink."

Jamie: "A drink? What are you talking about?"

Pat: "Drink—you know—the hard stuff. Let's check out my folks' liquor cabinet."

Jamie: "We'd get killed! Your parents are just like mine. They may let us drink a little wine on special occasions. But they'd never let us have a real drink. They think we're too young!"

Pat: "Sarah drinks her folks' liquor all the time. Lots of kids do it. They never get caught. Come on, what do you say?"

Thinking It Over

Read the following situations. Think about what you would do. Answer each question.

1. You like to watch Saturday morning cartoons with your younger brother and sister. Your friends say that only babies watch cartoons. Someone turns to you and says, "You still watch cartoons, don't you?" What will you say? _____

_____

_____

Why do you respond this way? _____

_____

_____

2. You are at the mall with three friends. The discussion turns to shoplifting. Each of them tells about having stolen something from a store, but you admit you never took anything from a store without paying for it. They pressure you to shoplift now—to go into the store and take a package of gum. What will you do? _____

_____

_____

Why do you respond this way? _____

_____

_____

3. Think about a recent example when you were pressured by your peers to do or not do something. What did they want you to do? _____

_____

_____

What did you decide to do? _____

_____

Why did you respond this way? _____

_____

The Yearbook Picture

TEACHER INFORMATION

Overview

Balancing individual rights with the rights of a group can be a delicate task. When are the two in conflict? When should one have more influence than the other? Samantha and Arlene have come to school with outrageously styled green hair. And it just happens to be the day that yearbook pictures are being taken.

Objectives

1. Consider group rights versus individual rights.
2. Compare opinions of parents, teachers, and students on a specific issue.

Preparation

Make one copy of each of the following pages of "The Yearbook Picture" for each student:

You Decide	School Uniforms
Activity Sheet	Thinking It Over

Presentation

Talk with students about "rights." What do they consider to be their "rights"? What are their "rights" as members of the school community? Is there any time when these "rights" are in conflict?

Samantha and Arlene encounter just such a conflict. They have to make a choice whether to insist on their personal "rights" and be excluded from a school activity or to give up their "rights" in order to participate. Distribute copies of "You Decide." Have students read the story.

Distribute copies of "Activity Sheet." Have students work in pairs to answer the questions. Discuss their answers as a class. How did students answer each of the questions?

Some schools require students to wear uniforms. Other schools are considering making this change. Some people think uniforms are a violation of individual rights of expression. Talk about this issue with the class. There are three major groups of people who will be affected by this issue: teachers, students, and parents. Distribute copies of "School Uniforms." Each student will talk with students, teachers, and parents to get their opinions about school uniforms. Discuss the results. Is their a consensus in any of the three groups?

Distribute copies of "Thinking It Over." Have students answer the questions and then discuss them together. Whose rights are more important?

You Decide

It was impossible not to notice Samantha and Arlene when they walked into school.

"You gotta look at this!" Marley nudged her friend.

Sandy was finishing some homework but looked up from her book at Marley's urging. "Wow!" she said and stared as Samantha and Arlene walked down the hall.

Everybody stared—teachers and students. All eyes were on Samantha and Arlene.

"Did you think it was Halloween?" someone called out.

"You forgot to take off your clown wigs!" yelled out another person.

But Samantha and Arlene just smiled, continued talking together, and walked to their homeroom.

The bell rang for school to begin, and the corridor emptied as students and teachers went to homeroom. The noise and commotion in the hall turned to silence.

"Good morning," the voice on the intercom sounded out over the static. Today the voice belonged to Mrs. O'Reilly, the yearbook advisor. "This morning the photographer is here to take yearbook pictures," she announced. "We will have an extended homeroom period while we take photographs of each homeroom class. You will be called room by room to the gym for your picture. Thank you for your cooperation."

Mrs. O'Reilly left the principal's office and headed down the hallway to room 10. She knocked on the door and then said to the homeroom teacher, "May I please speak with Samantha and Arlene for a minute?"

The girls joined Mrs. O'Reilly in the hall. "Good morning," she said to them. The girls smiled politely. "I see that you have changed your hairstyle today." The girls nodded. "What made you decide on this change?"

"Just trying it out," said Samantha.

"We wanted to do something a little different," added Arlene.

"Well, it certainly is different," agreed Mrs. O'Reilly. "But tell me, what made you choose today to wear your hair like this?"

"No reason," said Arlene.

"We were just hacking around last night and thought we'd try it," said Samantha.

"Well, today just happens to be yearbook picture day, and your hair doesn't seem appropriate for the yearbook."

"Why not?" asked Samantha.

"Yearbooks tell about the entire year and what happened at the school." Mrs. O'Reilly had been yearbook advisor for 15 years—she had very definite ideas about what should be in a yearbook. "I'm not sure green hair standing straight up from your head is something that this school should include in its yearbook!"

"Why not?" asked Arlene. "This is me and it's something I'm doing during this year. I'm part of this school."

"Yes, you are part of this school, and we want you to be included in the yearbook. But you cannot be in the picture the way you look right now. It wouldn't be fair to the rest of the school. We'll leave your class until last to photograph. You and Samantha have time to wash the color out of your hair and be ready for the picture."

"What if we don't wash our hair?" asked Samantha.

"Then you won't be in the picture of your homeroom in the yearbook," answered Mrs. O'Reilly. "It's that simple. You have a choice to make." She turned and walked down the hall toward the gymnasium.

Activity Sheet

1. What are some possible reasons Samantha and Arlene might have had for dying their hair? List as many reasons as you can.

_____

_____

_____

_____

_____

Which reason is the most likely? Put an X next to that reason.

2. What are some possible reasons Mrs. O'Reilly might have had for not wanting Samantha and Arlene in the yearbook with green hair? List as many reasons as you can.

_____

_____

_____

_____

_____

Which reason is the most likely? Put an X next to that reason.

3. If you were Samantha or Arlene and faced with this decision, what would you do? Explain your answer.

_____

_____

_____

_____

The Yearbook Picture
School Uniforms

Some schools require students to wear uniforms. How do *you* feel about uniforms? Do teachers, students, and parents have different opinions about school uniforms? Talk with two teachers, two students, and two parents to get their opinions.

	Good Idea	Bad Idea	Reasons
Parent #1	____	____	_____
			_____
			_____
Parent #2	____	____	_____
			_____
			_____
Student #1	____	____	_____
			_____
			_____
Student #2	____	____	_____
			_____
			_____
Teacher #1	____	____	_____
			_____
			_____
Teacher #2	____	____	_____
			_____
			_____

Name _____

Thinking It Over

1. If you were a classmate of Samantha and Arlene, would you want them to be pictured in the yearbook with their green hair? Why or why not?

   _____

   _____

   _____

2. Whose rights are more important?

   _____ Samantha's and Arlene's rights to dress as they want

   _____ The school's right to have a yearbook that looks nice

   Explain your answer:

   _____

   _____

   _____

3. Think about this situation. The school soccer games must be played on Saturday morning according to league rules. Todd moves into town. He is an excellent soccer player and wants to join the team. The team would welcome him as a member, but his family belongs to a religious community that worships on Saturday. They are threatening to sue the school unless games are changed to another time when Todd can play.

   What are Todd's rights?   What are the school's rights?

   _____   _____

   _____   _____

   _____   _____

   _____   _____

The Super Bowl Tickets

TEACHER INFORMATION

Overview

Friends are important. Everyone needs friends. And everyone needs to develop skills to be a good friend. Sometimes occasions arise when we have to make "Solomon-like" decisions between friends. Reggie, Sean, and Russell are the Three Musketeers. They have been best friends since second grade. Then Reggie is given the very special gift of a trip. But he can only invite one friend to accompany him.

Objectives

1. Evaluate several possible choices in a situation to determine whether or not they are good choices.
2. Identify qualities of friendship that are important.
3. Review decisions and their consequences when people have had to choose between friends.

Preparation

Make one copy of each of the following pages of "The Super Bowl Tickets" for each student:

You Decide   Thinking About Friends
Activity Sheet   Thinking It Over

Presentation

Talk with students about friendship. Have any of them had any long-standing friendships? What is the longest friendship any of the class members have had? Distribute copies of "You Decide." Have class members read to discover why Reggie has to choose between his two best friends.

Distribute copies of "Activity Sheet." Have students work individually or in small groups to consider several choices Reggie might make. When students have completed the activity sheet, discuss their answers together. What other possible choices did they suggest?

Talk with members of the class about qualities of friendship that are important. Distribute copies of "Thinking About Friends." Students work individually to finish each sentence. Allow students to share their sentences in a class discussion.

Distribute copies of "Thinking It Over." Students will complete the activity sheet. Divide the class into groups of three or four students to discuss their responses to the questions.

You Decide

The last gift in his Christmas stocking was small and flat. It looked like an envelope. Reggie picked up the package and read the tag attached to the ribbon. It was from his Uncle Matt. But that did not give him any clue about what was in the package. He looked at his uncle, but that was no help. Uncle Reggie just smiled at him.

Sometimes Reggie's uncle gave him money—it could be as little as $10 or as much as $50. And you couldn't even count on it being a gift you would want—his uncle could be quite a jokester. For his birthday one year, Uncle Matt had given him a year-long membership in Dial-A-Joke. It was really just Uncle Matt's phone number, and whenever Reggie called, his uncle would tell him a joke.

Everyone watched as Reggie opened Uncle Matt's gift. The family had a tradition of having just one person open a gift at a time. Sometimes it was nice to have all the attention. But it could be a little embarrassing if you didn't really like the gift—or didn't even quite know what it was. Even so, you had to pretend it was just what you wanted and say "thank-you" like you meant it.

Reggie removed the ribbon and wrapping paper. Just as he suspected, there was an envelope inside. Reggie opened the envelope and found three tickets. He looked at the tickets, and looked at his uncle, and then looked at the tickets again. He couldn't believe his eyes. They were Super Bowl tickets! He looked at the date—yes, they were for the upcoming game. "Is this a joke?" he asked.

"No, they're real!" his uncle assured him. "Three tickets to next month's Super Bowl!"

"Wow! This is fantastic!" No need to fake enthusiasm about this present! "Three tickets to the Super Bowl! I can't believe it. Thank you! Thank you! You're the best, Uncle Matt! This is great. Wait 'til I tell Sean and Russell. They won't believe it either! We're going to the Super Bowl!"

"I thought you'd like to bring a friend," said Matt. "That's why I got the extra ticket. It means we won't be able to stay in a motel. I just don't have enough money. These tickets were pretty expensive. We'll have to take sleeping bags and catch some shuteye in the car. But that's OK. So which friend are you going to invite to go with us?"

Reggie was puzzled. He looked again at the tickets in his hand. "What do you mean 'bring *a* friend'?" Reggie asked his uncle. "There are three tickets here. Doesn't that mean I can invite two friends to go to the game?"

"Now wait a minute—one ticket is for me," answered Uncle Matt. "I'm going to the game too. How do you think you're going to get there? It's a long drive! No, the tickets are for you and for me and for one friend of your choice. Who are you going to invite?"

"Just one friend? I can't invite just one friend. Sean and Russell and I are all best friends. I can't just invite one and not the other." Reggie was having trouble adjusting to this information. "Can't you get another ticket?"

"Do you have any idea how much these tickets cost me?" asked his uncle. "No, I can't get another ticket. They were sold out long ago. I thought you'd like to bring a friend and so I got three tickets instead of just two. But if you can't make the choice, then just forget it. I know plenty of people who would jump at the chance to go to the Super Bowl. If you don't want to go, I can take them."

"No, no . . . that's not what I meant." Reggie certainly wanted to go to the Super Bowl with his uncle. "It's just that I don't know who to invite. Sean and Russell and I have been best friends since second grade. We always do everything together. How can I invite one of them to go and not invite the other? How can I choose which one I will invite?"

Activity Sheet

1. After reading "You Decide," think about the decision Reggie has to make. Listed below are some possible choices Reggie could make. Read each choice. Is it a good choice or a bad choice? Explain.

good   bad
choice choice

☐ ☐   Reggie could invite Sean to go to the game and tell him not to tell Russell they are going.

_____

_____

☐ ☐   Reggie could stay home and give Sean and Russell the tickets to go with his uncle.

_____

_____

☐ ☐   Reggie could invite both Sean and Russell to go and hope they could buy a ticket there.

_____

_____

☐ ☐   Reggie could invite a cousin or another friend instead of either Russell or Sean.

_____

_____

2. Suggest another choice Reggie could make about the tickets. Do you think it is a good choice or a bad choice? Explain.

☐ ☐   _____

_____

_____

The Super Bowl Tickets

Thinking About Friends

What is important to you in your friendships? Finish each of the following sentences.

1. Friends always _____

_____.

2. Friends never _____

_____.

3. The most important quality I look for in a friend is _____

_____.

4. I know someone is my friend if _____

_____.

5. Everyone needs a friend because_____

_____.

6. I need a friend most when _____

_____.

7. I would be angry if a friend of mine _____

_____.

8. The hardest time to be a friend is when _____

_____.

9. My best friend _____

_____.

Thinking It Over

1. Reggie has a tough choice to make. What would you do if you were Reggie? Explain.

   _____

2. a. Think about a movie or TV show you have watched in which a character had to make a choice between two friends. Describe the situation.

   _____

   _____

   b. What choice did the character make?

   _____

   _____

   c. In your opinion, did this turn out to be the best choice? Why or why not?

   _____

   _____

3. a. Think of a time when you have had to make a choice between two friends. Describe the situation. How did you make your decision?

   _____

   _____

   b. Looking back, was it a good decision? What has happened to the friendships? What would you do now if faced with the same choice?

   _____

   _____

The Fight

Overview

The "Blame Game" is alive and well. On every side, we hear people saying, "It was the other person's fault." More often it seems people are unwilling to take responsibility for their actions and the events that follow. Glen and Owen got into a fight. Each could see what the other had done that was offensive. Neither could see his own personal responsibility.

Objectives

1. Identify responsibility of each member of an altercation.
2. Use an Action Plan for assessing personal behavior and identifying ways to change behavior.
3. List guidelines for behavior as given in the school handbook.

Preparation

Make one copy of each of the following pages of "The Fight" for each student:

You Decide	School Handbook
Action Plan	Thinking It Over
Activity Sheet	

Have copies available of the school handbook or another source for school behavior guidelines.

Presentation

Assign each student a partner. Distribute copies of "You Decide." In each pair, one student takes on the role of Glen and one student takes on the role of Owen. Students will read the story. This is not a role play. All students read the entire story, not just their own character's lines. As students read, ask them to be aware of how their character is thinking and feeling.

When students have finished the story, the teacher takes on the role of the principal. Owen and Glen have just been sent to the principal's office. Distribute a copy of "Action Plan" to each student. Ask each student to think about what has happened and to write down a personal Action Plan.

Now ask students to take on a new role. They each become one of the other students in the classroom with Owen and Glen. Distribute copies of "Activity Sheet." As students answer each question, they are given the next direction on the page. Discuss the activity to make certain students understand that only when someone accepts responsibility can an altercation be effectively ended.

Talk with students about school handbooks. Distribute copies of "School Handbook." Talk with students about the school's classroom behavior code.

Distribute copies of "Thinking It Over." Students will each complete an Action Plan that might have resulted from a personal fight or disagreement they have had.

You Decide

Glen got up to sharpen his pencil. When he returned to his desk, he saw Owen taking a homework paper out of his science book. "Hey, that's my paper!" said Glen. "Give it back!"

"I'm just looking at it. I wanted to see if you had the right answers," said Owen.

"As if you'd know the right answers! You're just too stupid to do the assignment yourself. Do your own work and give my paper back." Glen stood over Owen and reached for the paper. Owen turned and held the paper out of Glen's reach.

"Take your old paper," said Owen. Glen reached again for the paper, but Owen jerked it away. Glen fell against Owen's desk.

"Get away from my things," Owen spoke sharply. "Don't put your hands all over my desk."

Glen regained his balance. "I wouldn't touch your old desk if you'd just give back what's mine." Glen was angry and he punched Owen in the shoulder.

Owen dropped Glen's paper and stood up. "You hit me! That was a big mistake. No one hits me and gets away with it!"

Glen stepped back. He hadn't meant to get in a fight. He just wanted what was his. Owen grabbed Glen's arm. Glen kicked Owen in the shin. Every eye in the class was focused on Glen and Owen. Some students stood and moved closer to see the action.

Just then Mrs. Quimby returned to the room. She'd only gone to take some papers to the office and was back within two or three minutes. But she returned to find her classroom in an uproar. No one noticed her enter the room. "That will be enough!" she said in her sternest voice.

All noise in the classroom stopped. Glen and Owen stood apart, but continued glaring at each other. The remaining students returned silently to their seats.

"He took . . . ." Glen started to explain.

"He hit me . . . ." Owen defended himself at the same time.

But Mrs. Quimby interrupted. "I don't want to hear a word from either of you. Go to the principal's office." She pointed to the door. "This is unacceptable behavior. Get out!"

The Fight

Action Plan

Assume you are either Glen or Owen in the story. You get to the principal's office and are asked why you are there. You say that you were in a fight, and Mrs. Quimby sent you to the office. You are handed an Action Plan to complete and are directed to a desk. Fill out the Action Plan.

Action Plan

Student Name: _____ Sent by: _____

What were you doing that got you in trouble? (Situation)

What was the effect of your behavior on the class?

What problem did your behavior cause you?

Was the way you chose to behave a good choice? Yes ____ No ____

Why?

My Plan

In the future, I will _____

_____

What are you willing to do differently to make your plan work?

_____

What will you do to make certain you follow this plan?

_____

_____

Student Signature   Teacher Signature

Name _____

Activity Sheet

Assume you are a student in Mrs. Quimby's class. You were in the room and saw the fight between Owen and Glen. Answer the following questions.

1. Whom do you think started the fight?

   ☐ Glen (Go to Question #3.)   ☐ Owen (Go to Question #2.)

2. Owen says, "He hit me first. If Glen hadn't hit me, there wouldn't have been a fight." What do you say to Owen?

   ☐ "I guess you're right. Glen did start it." (Go to #3.)

   ☐ "Why did Glen hit you?" (Go to #4.)

3. Glen says, "Owen was a bully and took my paper. If he hadn't taken it, there wouldn't have been a fight."
   What do you say to Glen?

   ☐ "I guess you're right. Owen did start it." (Go to #2.)

   ☐ "How would hitting Owen get your paper back?" (Go to #5.)

4. Owen says, "No reason. I was looking at his paper to see how he answered the science questions. But I didn't hurt anything."
   What do you say to Owen?

   ☐ "That was no reason for Glen to hit you." (Go to #3.)

   ☐ "What would have happened if you had kept your hands off what did not belong to you?" (Go to #6.)

5. Glen says, "He would know I'm not going to let him bully me, and I'll stand up for my rights."
   What do you say to Glen?

   ☐ "You had every right to stick up for yourself." (Go to #2.)

   ☐ "What would have happened if you had kept your hands to yourself?" (Go to #6.)

6. He says, "There wouldn't have been a fight." (Go to #7.)

7. Whom do you think started the fight?
   ☐ Glen (Go to #3.)
   ☐ Owen (Go to #2.)
   ☐ Both (You're done!)

The Fight

School Handbook

The school handbook adopted by one middle school includes the following general behavior code for all classrooms:

a. Follow directions.
b. Be on time and prepared for class.
c. Remain seated; raise hand to speak.

d. Keep hands, feet, and objects to self.
e. Be respectful to all persons.

1. In the story, which part(s) of the behavior code did Owen fail to follow? Explain.

_____

_____

_____

2. In the story, which part(s) of the behavior code did Glen fail to follow? Explain.

_____

_____

_____

3. Look through your school handbook. What guidelines does your school have for classroom behavior?

_____

_____

_____

4. What are the consequences when students do not follow these guidelines?

_____

_____

_____

Thinking It Over

Think about a time when you have been in a fight or an angry disagreement that led to harsh words. It might have been in class or with a brother or sister or a friend. Complete the following Action Plan to help you think about what happened and what you can do to prevent a similar situation in the future.

1. What was the situation? _____

   _____

   _____

2. What did I do? _____

   _____

   _____

3. Why was my action a problem? _____

   _____

   _____

4. What is my plan to keep this problem from happening again? _____

   _____

   _____

5. What am I willing to do differently to make my plan work? _____

   _____

   _____

6. When am I going to make this change? _____

   _____

   _____

The Missing Money

Overview

Fairness is a very big issue for middle school students. But there is also a code of behavior that abhors "tattling" or "squealing." What happens when the two conflict? An entire class is being punished because of something done by an unknown person. Simon and Marty have a conversation with Derek that makes them suspicious he is involved.

Objectives

1. Distinguish between facts and suspicions.
2. Practice brainstorming to determine a course of action.
3. Explore personal feelings about when it is right to "inform" on an offender.

Preparation

Make one copy of each of the following pages of "The Missing Money" for each student:

    You Decide   Brainstorming

    Activity Sheet   Thinking It Over

Presentation

Talk with the class about being an "informant." When is it right to tell that others have done something wrong? Distribute copies of "You Decide." Read and think about what Simon and Marty should do.

What do Marty and Simon KNOW about the missing money? Why are they suspicious of Derek? Distribute copies of "Activity Sheet." Have students work in pairs to assess what are facts and what are suspicions.

What should Marty and Simon do? Talk about brainstorming. It is a helpful method for finding creative solutions to a difficult problem. Distribute copies of "Brainstorming." With students continuing to work in pairs, playing the roles of Marty and Simon, have them brainstorm possible courses of action for the boys. After brainstorming, what does each pair think Marty and Simon should do?

Distribute copies of "Thinking It Over." Allow students time to individually consider each situation. Then open the situation to a class discussion. Is it always "right" to tell when you know someone has done something wrong? What other circumstances have to be in place for each class member to think they would "tell"? Is there any consensus among the class members, or do their opinions vary?

You Decide

"Does anyone here have anything to say?" Mr. Jacobs looked around the classroom. There was a hush in the room and no one moved. It seemed like hardly anyone was even breathing.

Finally Mr. Jacobs spoke again. His voice was low and firm. "Well, we've got a problem. The money is missing. I'm quite sure someone in this room knows what happened to it." Mr. Jacobs was very angry. He continued to look around the room as he spoke, focusing on first one student and then another. The students sat silently, most keeping their eyes on Mr. Jacobs. A few looked down at their desks as they listened.

"Until that person or persons come forward, things are going to be a little different in this room. Instead of going outdoors at lunch break to be with your friends, I want you all to come back to homeroom. Bring your books and be prepared to spend the time studying. The pizza celebration on Friday is cancelled, and we'll . . . ."

Rinnnnnnnng. It was the school bell. Mr. Jacobs paused, but no one dared to move. "OK, class," Mr. Jacobs said at last. "That's all for today. You're dismissed to go home." The students filed quietly out of the classroom.

"That's not fair," Simon muttered under his breath as he shoved his books in his locker and grabbed his jacket. "I didn't take the money. I don't know anything about it. Why do I have to stay in and be punished?"

"We're all being punished enough, anyway," agreed Marty who had the locker next to Simon's. "The money belonged to all of us."

"Yeah—and without the money, we won't be able to go to the science museum either! This stinks!"

Marty and Simon headed for the door. Derek ran to catch up as they headed down the stairs. "Hey, let's stop by The Card Stop on our way home. Let's see if he has any new trading cards."

"Nah," said Simon. "I don't have any money to buy anything. Anyway, why are you in such a good mood? Didn't you hear what 'Jake-o' said?"

"Yeah, I'm bummed," said Marty. "He's keeping us in prison!"

"Oh, don't sweat the small stuff. He'll get over it. In just a few days, everything'll be back to normal. It's no big deal," added Derek.

"What do you mean 'small stuff'?" asked Marty. We must have had almost $300 collected. That's a lot of money. And now it's all gone. That *is* a big deal!"

"That's not so much for some of the kids in our class! Their parents will just kick in the money and we'll be on our way to the museum. Besides, 'Jake-o' shouldn't have left the money lying around. He's just taking it out on us because he was a jerk! 'Jerk-o' is what we should call him. That fits him," said Derek.

"What do you mean about his leaving the money lying around? How do you know that?" asked Marty. "Mr. Jacobs didn't say anything about where the money was."

"Oh sure he did," said Derek. "He told us he left it on the desk."

"No he didn't," Simon agreed with Marty. "He just said the money was missing. He didn't say anything about where he had put it."

"What's it matter?" demanded Derek. "Let's stop talking about it. This is depressing. Are you going with me to The Card Stop or not? I could loan you some money."

"Not today," said Simon.

"Me either," added Marty.

"Well, see you 'round," Derek left his friends and headed for the store. Marty and Simon continued on their way home.

"That was weird," said Marty. "How did he know Mr. Jacobs left the money on his desk?"

"Yeah, and where did he get money to spend on trading cards?" asked Simon. "He never has any money." Simon paused and then looked at his friend. "Are you thinking what I'm thinking?"

"I think Derek knows what happened to the money," agreed Marty. "But what can we do about it?"

Activity Sheet

Work with a partner to answer the questions below. One of you is Simon and one is Marty.

1. What did you learn from Mr. Jacobs about the missing money?

   _____

   _____

2. What things make you suspicious that Derek knows something about the missing money? Use a new line for each thing that makes you suspicious.

   _____

   _____

   _____

   _____

   _____

   _____

   _____

   _____

   _____

   _____

   _____

3. A FACT is something that can be proven to be true. Fact: "The money is missing."

   A SUSPICION is something believed without any proof. Suspicion: "I think Derek knows what happened to the money."

   Reread your answers in #2. Write an "F" next to each answer that is a FACT and an "S" next to each answer that is a suspicion.

The Missing Money
Brainstorming

Brainstorming is a way to come up with possible solutions for a difficult problem.

Continue to work with a partner. You are Simon and Marty. You think Derek knows something about the missing money. What can you do?

As fast as you can, write possibilities down the left side of this paper. Do not think about whether or not they are good ideas.

Brainstorming

_____   _____
_____   _____
_____   _____
_____   _____
_____   _____
_____   _____
_____   _____
_____   _____
_____   _____

Now go back and look at the ideas you generated. Which ones do you know right off won't work? Why? Which ideas are somewhat good? Are there parts of several ideas you can combine? Beside each idea, tell whether you think it is good or bad and why.

Talk with your partner. What do you think you should do?

_____
_____
_____
_____

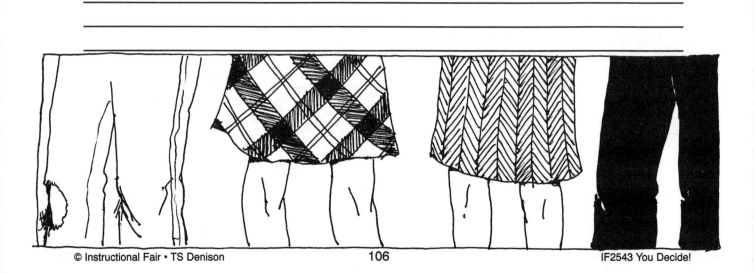

Thinking It Over

Over the weekend, someone painted graffiti all across the outside of a school bus. You know that your classmates Marley and Andrew did it. Think about each of the following

situations. What would you do?

1. The principal mentions the graffiti in the announcements and asks that anyone with information come to the office.

What do you do? _____

_____

Why? _____

_____

2. The two people who wrote the graffiti are your good friends.

What do you do? _____

_____

Why? _____

_____

_____

3. The principal offers a reward for anyone who has information about the vandalism.

What do you do? _____

_____

Why? _____

_____

4. A person is accused of writing the graffiti, but you know it is the wrong person.

What do you do? _____

_____

Why? _____

_____

_____

5. The principal announces that all sports are cancelled until the "graffiti-crime" is solved.

What do you do? _____

_____

Why? _____

_____

_____

6. The two people who painted the bus threaten to harm you if you tell.

What do you do? _____

_____

Why? _____

_____

_____

A Fourth for Lunch

Overview

Discrimination is a fact of life. Even as we see and condemn discrimination in our society, we blindly practice other forms of discrimination in our day-to-day lives. Emily has just given a report on Rosa Parks. She and her classmates criticize the policy that forced black people to sit at the back of the bus. But what do their actions show?

Objectives

1. Compare people's words that condemn discrimination with their actions.
2. List various reasons people are discriminated against.
3. Identify specific incidents of discrimination.

Preparation

Make one copy of each of the following pages of "A Fourth for Lunch" for each student:

      You Decide   Discrimination

      Activity Sheet   Thinking It Over

Have available local newspapers and magazines.

Note: students will need to go to the library to use *The Reader's Guide to Periodical Literature.*

Presentation

Talk with members of the class about discrimination. Does anyone know about Rosa Parks and how she experienced discrimination? Distribute copies of "You Decide." This is a story of three girls who were quite critical of the discrimination experienced by Rosa Parks.

Have students work in pairs as they think about the story. Distribute copies of "Activity Sheet." Students will answer the questions.

Talk with students about *The Reader's Guide to Periodical Literature.* Be certain students know how to use it to find magazine articles. Distribute copies of "Discrimination." Students will need library time to complete the activity sheet.

Discuss various articles students researched. What varieties of discrimination did they encounter?

Distribute copies of "Thinking It Over." Have available local newspapers and magazines for students to find articles that illustrate incidents of discrimination in their own community. Allow students time to answer the questions and then discuss those answers together.

You Decide

Emily picked up her tray and looked around the cafeteria. It took just a few moments to spot Lisa and Heidi sitting at a table by the windows.

"Have a seat." Heidi greeted her friend and pushed out a chair as Emily approached their table.

"Boy, am I glad that's done!" Emily placed her lunch tray on the table and dropped down on the seat. She had just come from giving a report in social studies class. "I get so nervous when I have to stand up in front of the class."

"As if you have anything to be nervous about," observed Lisa. "You always give one of the best reports."

"Yeah," agreed Heidi. "Yours is the best one so far this time, too. But I never heard of that lady." The class was studying the second half of the twentieth century in the United States. Everyone had to choose one person from the teacher's list and then research how that person had affected history. Emily had chosen Rosa Parks.

"I don't know why it matters where people sit on the bus!" said Lisa.

"Me either. Everyone should be able to sit anywhere they want," said Emily.

Heidi had been looking over the shoulders of the other two girls. She interrupted their conversation. "Don't look now—but here comes that new girl—what's her name?"

"Do you mean Geneva?" asked Emily. "She's the one who always wears those weird clothes. What does she want?"

"Maybe she'll want to sit with us," suggested Lisa.

"Oooo, she's so strange," said Heidi. "I guess her whole family is kind of strange. My father says they have a zillion kids."

"She's in my homeroom," said Emily. "She won't salute the flag with the others in the morning."

"If she wants to sit here, we can just tell her the seat is saved for Abbey," suggested Lisa.

"But Abbey isn't in school today!" noted Emily.

"So? What does that matter?" asked Heidi. "Geneva is new in school. She'll never know Abbey isn't here."

"Besides," explained Lisa, "Abbey usually does sit with us."

"Shhh," hissed Heidi. "She's getting close and she'll hear what we're saying."

Geneva approached the table where the girls were sitting. "May I sit here?" she asked shyly. "The lunch room is really full today. There don't seem to be many places to sit."

"This seat is taken," answered Lisa. "No, you can't sit here."

"Our friend Abbey always sits with us at lunch," added Emily.

"I know. I've seen the four of you on other days. You seem to be very good friends. The chair was empty, and I thought she might be away," explained Geneva.

"We always sit together," Heidi echoed the words of her friends.

"OK," said Geneva. "I'll look for another place."

Activity Sheet

1. Who was Rosa Parks? What single action of hers made her famous? (If you do not know, look in an encyclopedia to answer the question.)

   _____

   _____

   _____

   _____

   _____

2. How would you define the word *discrimination*?

   _____

   _____

   _____

3. In the story, "A Fourth for Lunch," what words or actions make you think Emily and her friends are against discrimination?

   _____

   _____

   _____

   _____

4. What words or actions make you think Emily and her friends think discrimination is OK?

   _____

   _____

   _____

A Fourth for Lunch
Discrimination

1. Rosa Parks was discriminated against because of her color. There are many other reasons why people may be discriminated against. Look up the word *discrimination* in *The Reader's Guide to Periodical Literature*. What types of discrimination do you find listed there?

   _____

   _____

   _____

   _____

2. Select one article. Find the magazine and read the article. Tell what you learned. What was the basis for discrimination? How was the discrimination shown? How were people hurt by discrimination?

   _____

   _____

   _____

   _____

   _____

   _____

   _____

   _____

   _____

   _____

   _____

   _____

3. What suggestions do you have for overcoming the discrimination you read about?

   _____

   _____

   _____

Thinking It Over

1. Look through a local newspaper or magazine to find an article about a person or group of people being discriminated against. Write a summary of the article: who? what? when? where? why? how?

   _____

   _____

   _____

   _____

2. Sometimes people discriminate against students because of their youth. Tell about a time you experienced age discrimination or were discriminated against for some other reason. How did you feel?

   _____

   _____

   _____

3. When have you discriminated against another person or group of people? What happened? What caused the incident? How might you behave differently if faced with that situation in the future?

   _____

   _____

   _____

   _____

   _____

   _____

The Dance

TEACHER INFORMATION

Overview

Fear can be healthy. There are terrible dangers in the world, and fear can help us avoid situations where danger and evil lurk. But sometimes our fears bind us and prevent our trying something new. Sherri has worked hard to make the school dance a success, but her fears about something she has never done keep her from joining in the dance.

Objectives

1. Identify personal fears.
2. List specific fears that make it hard to face new situations.

Preparation

Make one copy of each of the following pages of "The Dance" for each student:

    You Decide   Thinking It Over

    Activity Sheet

Presentation

Talk with students about school dances. Does everybody like to go? What are the reasons some students enjoy dances? Why do others avoid school dances? Distribute copies of "You Decide." Read about two friends who are working hard on preparations for the spring dance.

Distribute copies of "Activity Sheet." Students can work with a partner to answer the questions. When students finish their work, have one person take the role of Sherri and another person take the role of Val. Role-play a conversation the two girls might have about the dance. If there is time, have two boys do a role play with one trying to convince his friend to come to the dance.

Help students face new situations by naming the things in new situations which are most scary. Distribute copies of "Thinking It Over." The first situation is from the story about Sherri and Val. Answer the questions together as a class. Have students work in pairs to complete #2 and #3. Each student will answer #4.

Conclude with a class discussion. Encourage students to talk about situations or experiences which are fearful for them. Explore ways to face those fears.

You Decide

A ringing the telephone interrupted the dinner conversation at the Farley home. "I'll get it!" Sherri jumped up from the table. "I'm finished anyway."

"Don't you want dessert?" her mother asked. The phone rang again.

"No, I've had enough to eat," Sherri said and hurriedly left the table.

"Can I have her piece of cake?" Sherri heard her little brother ask as she reached the phone.

"Hello." She picked up the receiver just as a third ring began.

"Hi Sherri. It's me, Val," said the voice on the line.

"Hi Val. I knew it would be you." Sherri had the portable phone. She took it into the bathroom and shut the door. Val was her best friend, and Sherri wanted privacy for their conversation.

"Aren't the decorations fabulous?" Sherri and Val had just spent the afternoon together working on decorations for the spring dance. Val continued to rave, "Especially that mural you are painting. It's beautiful. You are so talented."

"I like to paint," agreed Sherri.

"It's gorgeous! It's just going to make the whole dance. This is going to be the best spring dance ever! Everyone says so." Val was very enthusiastic.

"I'm glad," said Sherri.

"And those table decorations you showed us how to make! They're just right!"

"You guys are doing a good job. They're looking pretty good," agreed Sherri.

"I just wish you were going to go to the dance," said Val. "You should come. Won't you please come?"

"No, I'm not going," answered Sherri.

"But why?" asked Val. "You've worked the hardest of anyone to make it a success! It'll be fun! Why have you been working so hard on the dance if you don't want to come?"

There was silence on the line. Sherri did not answer.

"Why aren't you saying anything?" asked Val. "Come on, I'm your best friend. You can tell me. Why aren't you going to the dance?"

Sherri spoke very quietly. "I've never been to a dance before."

"So? Come to this one!" said Val. "It'll be a perfect first dance."

"But I can't . . . ."

"What do you mean, 'You can't'?" Val interrupted her friend. "Of course you can come."

"No, you don't understand. I can't . . . I can't dance."

"Well that's no problem! I can teach you. Come over to my house and we'll . . . ."

"No!" Sherri interrupted. "That's not all. What if nobody will dance with me? I'd just stand around all night and it would be so embarrassing."

"But that won't happen," Val tried to be reassuring. "Plenty of guys will want to dance with you."

"You're just saying that. And besides, I wouldn't know what to wear or how to act," protested Sherri. "Don't try to talk me into it. You're wasting your time. I can't go to the dance."

Name _____

The Dance

Activity Sheet

1. After reading the story, "The Dance," how would you describe Sherri's feelings about going to the dance? _____
_____

2. Give three examples of Sherri's words or behavior that explain your answer in #1.

   a. _____

   b. _____

   c. _____

3. Does Sherri really want to go to the dance? Yes _____ No _____
Explain your answer. _____
_____
_____
_____

4. What suggestions do you have for Val? Is there anything she can do to help her friend overcome her fears?
_____
_____
_____

5. What suggestions do you have for Sherri? _____
_____
_____

Thinking It Over

Facing new experiences or challenges can be scary. One helpful technique is to imagine all the bad things that might happen. Having already faced the worst, it is easier to confront the actual new experience.

Look at the people facing new experiences. What is the worst that could happen in each situation? Why should the person go ahead?

1. Sherri is afraid to go to the dance.
Bad things that might happen:

_____
_____
_____

Sherri should go because

_____
_____
_____
_____
_____

2. Tom is thinking about running for class president.
Bad things that might happen:

_____
_____
_____

Tom should run because

_____
_____
_____
_____
_____

3. Mark wishes he dared to go to Paris with the French Club.
Bad things that might happen:

_____
_____
_____

Mark should go because

_____
_____
_____
_____
_____

4. I am considering _____
Bad things that might happen:

_____
_____
_____

I should do it because

_____
_____
_____
_____
_____

The Disappointment

Overview

Is there anyone who has not experienced disappointment? When a person becomes disappointed, it is necessary to acknowledge the situation and experience the feelings. It is also important to avoid getting mired in past disappointment. Mitch did not make the hockey team; that is a disappointment. But his father assures him there is a whole world of opportunity awaiting.

Objectives

1. Acknowledge personal disappointments.
2. Identify personal interests and skills.
3. Assess volunteer or other opportunities for getting involved in the community.
4. Research ways others use their skills and interests in school and in the community.

Preparation

Make one copy of each of the following pages of "The Disappointment" for each student:

You Decide	Checklist for Getting Involved
Activity Sheet	Thinking It Over
Volunteer opportunities and community calendar from local paper	

Presentation

Talk with the class about disappointments. Who in the class has experienced a disappointment? What did they do to get past the disappointment and continue with their lives?

Distribute copies of "You Decide." Read the story to learn about Mitch's disappointment and how he is handling it.

Mitch's father showed him a list of activities from the local newspaper. Distribute copies of "Activity Sheet." Look through these activities to see what Mitch might choose to do.

How do people find new ways to use their interests or get involved in the community? Distribute copies of "Checklist for Getting Involved." Have students work individually to assess their own skills and interests and inventory opportunities available.

Have students interview one another to learn how their classmates use their skills at school and in the community. Have copies of local newspapers available. They usually contain calendars of events in the community and listings of volunteer possibilities. Students can refer to these listings as they plan how they can use their talents and interests in the world.

You Decide

Mitch sat in the den, sprawled on the recliner. The TV blared from the corner and Mitch stared at the screen. His dad came to the door, holding a newspaper under his arm. "Mind if I join you?" he asked.

"Suit yourself," said Mitch, never taking his eyes from the TV screen.

Mr. Hogan sat down on the couch. He watched the TV for a minute or two, then turned on the reading light next to him, opened his paper, and began to read.

When a commercial interrupted the TV show, Mr. Hogan peered over the paper at his son. Mitch's eyes still focused on the TV. "How's everything going, son?"

Mitch shrugged, "OK, I guess."

"Things at school OK?"

"Yeah . . . ."

"You seem to be watching a lot of TV these days."

"Nothin' else to do."

"I thought you were going to try out for the hockey team." Mitch's favorite sport was hockey, and he had been looking forward to playing on the school team this year.

"Yeah."

"When are the tryouts?" Mr. Hogan was puzzled by Mitch's attitude.

Just then the commercial ended. Mitch avoided his father's question. "I'm trying to watch this show, Dad."

"All right, we'll talk about it later." Mr. Hogan returned to his paper. But he kept one ear tuned to the television. Something was wrong. Mitch didn't usually watch this much television. He preferred to be with his friends or playing sports. Mr. Hogan wanted to talk with his son.

When the final credits began to roll for the show Mitch had been watching, Mr. Hogan laid down his paper. "So when *are* the hockey tryouts?" he asked.

"It doesn't matter. It's just a stupid game."

"Maybe so, but I asked you when the tryouts are—and I expect an answer."

"Last week."

"I didn't know they had already happened. How'd it go?"

"Not so hot . . . I didn't make the team."

"What?" Mr. Hogan was truly surprised.

"There were a whole lot of eighth graders and they got picked first. There can only be one team this year, and there weren't many places left."

"I still thought you would have made the team. You're a good player."

"I didn't. Sam and Casey and Eric and Ginny all got picked."

"Ginny's playing?"

"Yeah, girls can play now, too."

"But you can't? You didn't get picked for the team?"

"No." Mitch paused. "It's OK. It doesn't matter."

"Well, it does matter," said his father. "It's disappointing. If I were you, I'd be really upset." Mitch didn't answer. "So what are you going to do instead?"

Mitch shrugged. "What can I do? I wanted to play hockey. There's nothing else to do."

"I think I know how you must be feeling, son. It probably will take you a while to get past your disappointment. But when you do, maybe you can find some other activity that will be of interest to you. Look at this list of things to do right here in this paper. There's plenty to do and plenty of people who need you, believe me."

Activity Sheet

1. In the story, "The Disappointment," what behaviors show that Mitch is disappointed about not making the hockey team?

_____

_____

2. Read the classified ads below and then answer the questions.

Outdoors

Mountain Sports at the Mall presents its winter clinic series, offering hikes and skiing. Free. For more info, call 555-2961.

Outdoor Adventure Club meets first Tuesday of every month at Pine Hill School at 7 p.m. We offer winter hiking, snowshoeing, camping, ice climbing, and other trips for people of all skill levels.

Speed Skating Club holds weekly practices at the University Ice Arena Sundays at 4 p.m. Cost $5. Any skates will do.

Volunteer

ASA Network seeks host families for foreign exchange students ages 12-15. All speak English and will stay for summer months. 555-1029.

Buy Pollution. Pollution allowances are bought and sold just like other commodities. You can buy and retire allowances to prevent businesses from further pollution. For information, call 555-3610.

Clearview Nursing Home seeks volunteers to read stories, play games, go on outings, share a pet, and otherwise enrich the life quality of residents. 555-6691.

Community Health Services seeks volunteers to do office work. Call 555-0602.

Emergency Food Pantry seeks donations of non-perishable food items. 555-5885.

Memorial Library welcomes volunteers to shelve books, read to young patrons, and check out books. 555-2272.

Youth Center needs young people who skate to assist coaches of pee-wee teams. For details, call 555-8319.

From what you know about Mitch, find two ads that might be of interest to him. Why might he like doing these things?

_____

_____

_____

Name _____

The Disappointment
Checklist for Getting Involved

Complete the following checklist to help you think about ways you can get involved in your community.

About Me

1. I like to be ___ indoors ___ outdoors

2. I like to be ___ by myself ___ with others

3. I like to be with ___ young people ___ adults ___ older people ___ children

4. I like to
   - ___ read
   - ___ cook
   - ___ swim
   - ___ write
   - ___ sew
   - ___ listen
   - ___ baby-sit
   - ___ dance
   - ___ sing
   - ___ entertain
   - ___ garden
   - ___ play sports
   - ___ work with wood
   - ___ _____
   - ___ _____

5. I have ___ free hours a day   ___ free hours a week

Opportunities

6. My town has the following:
   - ___ community newspaper
   - ___ library
   - ___ hospital
   - ___ community center
   - ___ day care center
   - ___ playground
   - ___ nursing home
   - ___ youth organizations (scouts, 4-H, etc.)
   - ___ _____
   - ___ _____

7. People who could use my help with housework or running errands:
   - ___ Elderly neighbors (_____)
   - ___ People with disabilities (_____)
   - ___ Family with young children (_____)

8. Ways I could raise money for a good cause:
   - ___ bottle drive
   - ___ bake sale
   - ___ car wash
   - ___ put on a show
   - ___ yard work

Thinking It Over

1. Talk with two friends in your class. What are their interests? What do they like to do? How are they involved at school? In the community?

   a. Friend #1:_____

   _____

   _____

   _____

   _____

   _____

   _____

   _____

   b. Friend # 2: _____

   _____

   _____

   _____

   _____

   _____

   _____

   _____

2. How are you involved at school? In the community?_____

   _____

   _____

   _____

3. Think about the checklist you completed about getting involved. What other ideas does that give you about ways you can be active in your community?

   _____

   _____

   _____